TIMI

HORSES 1

2024/25 JUMPS SEASON

with **SPORTING LIFE**

CW01667785

CONTENTS

ISBN 978-1-8380349-8-6 Price £10.95

Printed and bound by
Weatherbys Ltd
Sanders Road
Wellingborough
NN8 4BX

SECTION 1

Timeform's Fifty To Follow, carefully chosen by Timeform and Sporting Life editorial staff, are listed below with their respective page numbers. A selection of ten (**marked in bold with a ★**) is made for those who prefer a smaller list.

The form summary for each horse is shown after its age, colour, sex and pedigree. The summary shows the distance, the state of the going and where the horse finished in each of its races since the start of the 2023/24 season. Performances are in chronological sequence with the date of its last race shown at the end (F-ran on Flat).

The distance of each race is given in furlongs. Steeplechase form figures are prefixed by the letter 'c', hurdle form figures by the letter 'h' and NH Flat race or bumper form figures by the letter 'b'.

The going is symbolised as follows: f–firm, m–good to firm; g–good, d–good to soft; s–soft; v–heavy.

Placings are indicated, up to the sixth place, by use of superior figures, an asterisk being used to denote a win and superior letters are used to convey what happened to a horse during the race: F–fell, pu–pulled up, ur–unseated rider, bd–brought down, su–slipped up, ro–ran out.

The Timeform Rating of a horse is simply the merit of the horse expressed in pounds and is arrived at by careful examination of its running against other horses. The ratings range from 175+ for the champions down to a figure of around 55 for selling platers. Symbols attached to the ratings: 'p'–likely to improve; 'P'–capable of much better form; '+'–the horse may be better than we have rated it.

Authentic Legacy h106p

4 bl.g. Authorized (Ire) – Forever Present (Ire) (Presenting)
2023/24 b14s^4 b16.3d h16d^2 Apr 13

Just days after I Am Maximus won the Grand National in April, his younger full brother All Authorized was successful too, albeit in much more lowly company in a maiden hurdle at Fontwell. All Authorized's success for Gary Moore came in the colours of Steve Packham, best known as the owner of the stable's very talented but enigmatic hurdler Goshen who gained a first win over fences at Exeter the previous month. Like All Authorized, Goshen is a son of the 2007 Derby and Juddmonte International winner Authorized, a stallion the Moore stable has evidently latched onto as he's also the sire of their promising four-year-old Authentic Legacy.

He was highly tried in a couple of bumpers, both of which were won by other members of our *Fifty*. Cheltenham's listed junior bumper on New Year's Day was no easy race for Authentic Legacy's debut but he was one of the better types in appearance, being a tall, useful-looking gelding, and he attracted support too. His inexperience was evident in the race but he showed plenty of ability in fourth, five lengths behind winner Kel du Large. Authentic Legacy wasn't seen out again until Newbury in late-March when he contested the valuable Goffs UK Spring Sale Bumper. He was more clued up this time but ran to a similar level as he had at Cheltenham, finishing in mid-division in the big field behind Regent's Stroll. His hurdling debut came at Chepstow the following month in a junior hurdle where he probably did well to finish second the way the race was run. Held up in rear, he proved no match for the odds-on favourite Knight of Allen who won readily from the front but Authentic Legacy kept on to be beaten just under five lengths.

Authentic Legacy, who was bought for £85,000 as a three-year-old, has three winning half-sisters, including fair hurdlers Kay Tara Tara and Presenting Nelly who were both successful last season, for Alan King and Dan Skelton respectively, and both of whom stay two and a half miles. Their dam Forever Present and grandam Sidalcea both gained their only wins in bumpers, but the latter was a half-sister to triple Gold Cup winner Best Mate, so Authentic Legacy has the pedigree, as well as the looks, of one who will win races over jumps. ***Gary & Josh Moore***

Conclusion: *Scopey four-year-old who shaped well on his hurdling debut after being highly tried in a couple of bumpers and will improve for that experience*

Ballee (Ire) h139

5 b. or br.g. Sageburg (Ire) – Spartan Angel (Ire) (Beneficial)

2023/24 h15.2s^{3} h16.5d* h16.5d* h16s^{ur} h16.5s^{2} :: 2024/25 h15.7m^{pu} May 11

The Alder Hey Handicap Hurdle, for conditional and amateur riders, at Aintree's Grand National Festival was a fiercely-run affair this year and was won in remarkable style by El Jefe who came from the clouds to overhaul Ballee and score by a length and a half. But the runner-up, who had raced keenly and taken up the running at the fourth flight, did really well under the circumstances and can have that effort marked up. One especially pleasing aspect of the performance, and something that's sure to stand him in good stead, was the fantastic attitude he displayed to briefly claw his way back into the lead on the run-in, only for one who had raced well off the pace to overhaul him close home.

Taking a strong hold is a trait of this horse and he lives on his nerves, but the talent is there for all to see. He won a novice hurdle at Taunton in November despite pulling hard and failing to jump with fluency and then, with a hood added, followed up with a wide-margin win at the same venue a couple of weeks later, showing all the raw materials of a horse who could make into a really smart performer. Incidentally, the runner-up from that first Taunton novice, Matterhorn, has shown smart form since going chasing and won his first four starts over fences, while the third home, Go To War, won both subsequent starts over hurdles last season.

Ballee's campaign ended on a low note when pulled up in the Swinton Handicap Hurdle at Haydock in May, but that came only four weeks after his Aintree slog and he was probably still feeling the effects of such a big effort. He'll benefit from his summer

Ballee (red sleeves) showed a fine attitude when runner-up at Aintree

break and, as a tall, useful-looking gelding, will be one to watch out for when sent novice chasing in the autumn. Novice handicap chases will be an option given his Aintree effort showed he's clearly on a competitive mark, but he could be some sight if allowed his head over fences and it would be little surprise were he to make his mark in better company. ***Philip Hobbs & Johnson White***

Conclusion: *Showed plenty of ability over hurdles and impressed with attitude when runner-up at Aintree; has a style that could make him a formidable opponent over fences*

Be Aware (Fr) h128

5 gr.g. Martaline – Kendova (Fr) (Kendor (Fr))

2023/24 h16.3s* h16s^2 h21d^2 h16g^2 Apr 27

The sight of another grey horse running in Andrew Cohen's blue and white colours will bring back memories for many of the top-class chaser Suny Bay. Trained for much of his career first by Charlie Brooks and then by Simon Sherwood, Suny Bay won several good staying handicap chases, notably the 1997 Hennessy Gold Cup, and ran in two Cheltenham Gold Cups, but will also be remembered for some sterling efforts in the Grand National which he contested four times. He was a remote second off a light weight in Lord Gyllene's National on his first attempt but a year later was runner-up again under the burden of 12-0 in a gruelling edition won by Earth Summit.

The Grand National is a long way off for Be Aware who has just completed his novice hurdle season but he's a raw-boned gelding and the type to make a chaser in due course. He looked potentially useful right from his very first start which came at Newbury in January. Sent off at 11/1 in a big field of maidens, he came from an unpromising position to overhaul one of the better-fancied runners, Navajo Indy, late on to win by two and a quarter lengths with a big gap to the rest. Be Aware duly improved on that initial effort though found one too good on each of his three remaining starts. On his next two outings, Be Aware finished well clear of the rest when going down by a neck to Yellow Star in a novice at Lingfield, conceding plenty of weight to the winner, and when beaten a length by Kamsinas, in receipt of weight this time, in a similar event at Kempton but over a longer trip. On his final start at Sandown in April, Be Aware contested one of the most competitive novice handicaps of the whole season and ran another good race, taking time to find full stride back down in trip but keeping on well on the run-in to be beaten a length by Helnwein.

As well as being a brother to the same connections' useful hurdler/chaser Lac de Constance, Be Aware is out of a half-sister to the 2020 'French Champion Hurdle' winner Paul's Saga, she too by Be Aware's sire Martaline. There are probably more races to be won with him over hurdles before he goes chasing. ***Dan Skelton***

Conclusion: *Lightly-raced chasing type who ended the season finishing second in a very competitive novice handicap; can win more races over hurdles before tackling fences*

Below The Radar (Ire) h127p

6 b.g. Getaway (Ger) – Benfaithful (Ire) (Beneficial)
2023/24 b16s* h21.7d* h19.9v* Mar 16

Below The Radar looks capable of grabbing people's attention if progressing as we expect this season. He's been patiently handled so far but has won all three starts under Rules despite looking like a work in progress who should continue to develop with experience.

Below The Radar showed an encouraging amount of speed for one with a staying pedigree and a pointing background (placed both times in that sphere) when winning on his bumper debut at Chepstow in November, beating an Irish point winner who subsequently landed a Haydock bumper with ease. Connections decided there was little point spending more time in bumpers with one bred to flourish over jumps and Below The Radar's next appearance came in a two-and-three-quarter mile novice hurdle at Hereford in January. The runner-up, who had finished placed on three

Below The Radar (white cap) has a bit of growing up to do but is blessed with ability

previous starts over hurdles, was ridden to bring stamina and jumping experience into play and he was much more fluent than Below The Radar who was slow at the first and continued to lose ground in the air. But raw ability—very raw in this case—was enough to see Below The Radar through.

He then produced a very similar display when following up in another novice hurdle at Uttoxeter on Midlands Grand National day, beating three previous winners. Sloppy jumping again hindered Below The Radar but he found a good leap when he needed it at the final flight and, as was the case at Hereford, he proved strong on the run-in to assert close home. He clearly has some growing up to do but it's really encouraging that he's unbeaten under Rules despite showing such obvious signs of inexperience and he's a bright prospect for chasing. ***Paul Nicholls***

Conclusion: *Still a work in progress but has shown a big engine to overcome a couple of novicey rounds of jumping over hurdles; likely to carry on progressing as he gains experience*

Bertie's Ballet **h123**

6 b.g. Albaasil (Ire) – More Ballet Money (Old Vic)
2023/24 h16v^{2} h15.7v* h15.6d^{2} h18.1s^{4} h20.5d^{3} Apr 20

Bertie's Ballet became Dianne Sayer's first ever bumper winner when making a successful debut at Newcastle in March 2022 and he went on to contest a total of five such events, recording his other win in that sphere at Kelso a year later in a race worth more than £15,000 to the winner. While he finished down the field in Aintree's Grade 2 bumper later that spring, Bertie's Ballet performed with credit against some good horses when switched to hurdles last term. One of those was Alan King's subsequent Scottish Champion Hurdle winner Favour And Fortune who had Bertie's Ballet three lengths back in second when the latter was given a considerate debut over hurdles at Wetherby in November.

Bertie's Ballet had no trouble in going one better the following month in a novice at Haydock, winning with a fair bit more in hand than the margin of a length and a half would suggest when beating main market rival Norman Fletcher. Improving on that, Bertie's Ballet chased home Paul Nicholls' Panjari in the Scottish Supreme Novices' Hurdle at Musselburgh and showed further progress upped in trip on his last couple of starts. He couldn't trouble some at least useful rivals in the Grade 2 Premier Novices' Hurdle at Kelso, especially after getting caught up in a melee at the first, but he ran well for fourth behind Personal Ambition who got the better of Grade 1 winner and fellow *Fifty* member Jango Baie. On his final start in a novice at Ayr on Scottish Grand National day, Bertie's Ballet's jumping let him down but he rallied from well back to claim an unlikely third, ten lengths behind Willie Mullins' exciting prospect Quai de Bourbon

Baileys Concerto, who once won seven races in a calendar year, and Tonto's Spirit, who holds the record for most wins at Cartmel, are two of the best jumpers Sayer has had. But there's a good chance Bertie's Ballet, who already has a Timeform rating of 123 after his novice hurdle season, will establish himself as the best she's trained, especially when he goes over fences. ***Dianne Sayer***

Conclusion: *Dual bumper winner who wasn't far behind some very good novices from much bigger yards in his first season over hurdles and is likely to make at least as good a chaser*

Best Life (Ire) **h100p**

6 b.g. Leading Light (Ire) – Gli Gli (Ire) (Supreme Leader)
2023/24 h20.6v^{4} h21.2v h19.4v^{3} h24.3d^{2} Mar 30

Best Life is one of the lowest-rated inclusions in this edition of Horses To Follow but he's also one of the least exposed which means there's plenty of scope for progress.

Best Life is by Gold Cup winner Leading Light and out of a three-mile hurdle winner whose best progeny also stayed three miles, so his pedigree is all about stamina. With that in mind, it's perhaps unsurprising that Best Life failed to make an impact in three starts in maiden and novice hurdles at around two and a half miles, though he did offer some encouragement on the third of those outings at Doncaster where he was no match for the two principals but was clearly best of the rest.

Best Life duly relished the step up in trip to three miles on his handicap debut at Haydock in March but he had the misfortune of bumping into a much-improved One Big Bang—who is also in the *Fifty*—on that horse's first start for James Owen. Irish recruit One Big Bang landed a gamble in style, but there was still a lot to like about Best Life's performance as he was the only one who even threatened to lay down a meaningful challenge to the winner in the straight before ultimately being brushed aside on the run to the final flight.

That was an encouraging display from Best Life and there should be races to be won with him if kept over hurdles, but as a tall, well-made gelding he has the physique of one who should thrive over fences. He also comes from a pointing background and was first past the post in such an event at Sandon though was later disqualified. ***Mel Rowley***

Conclusion: *Low-key start over hurdles but shaped well on his handicap debut behind a thrown-in rival; a switch to chasing could unlock further improvement*

Big John Wayne (Ire) h113p

6 b.g. Shantou (USA) – Balwaney (Fr) (Exit To Nowhere (USA))
2023/24 h21.7d^3 h20.3s^F Feb 24

There may have been no Grand National success to boost the stable's earnings last season, but the Lucinda Russell yard still crossed the million pounds threshold again and was in the top ten by prize-money as well as number of winners. Indeed, her personal best tally of 75, one more than that achieved by Donald McCain last season, was the highest among trainers based in the north of England or Scotland. One who looked unlucky not to contribute to that tally but is expected to do so this time around is Big John Wayne. He made only two appearances last term but showed plenty of promise in a couple of novice hurdles in the winter, starting out at Hereford in January, well away from Russell's main base in Scotland but close to the stable's satellite yard run by Tom Scudamore. Sent off at 14/1, Big John Wayne shaped like a stayer, getting outpaced two out after taking closer order and then keeping on to be beaten around ten lengths into third behind the promising Below The Radar. Big John Wayne faced just three rivals at Newcastle the following month, including the odds-on Moon Chime, a dual bumper who had got off the mark over hurdles at Huntingdon the previous month. Making the running this time, Big John Wayne was still in front, just over a length up on the favourite and looking the winner, when taking a heavy fall, leaving Moon Chime a long way clear.

A strong-galloping sort, Big John Wayne, as his name suggests, is a fine stamp of an individual, big and lengthy, who looks just the type to take to fences. He was also a late faller on his debut in Irish points but landed the odds on his only subsequent start in that sphere last October. Two of his half-brothers are also winning pointers and one of those, Mr Josiey Wales, was also a fairly useful three-mile hurdle winner in Ireland before joining Russell's stable last season. Their dam is an unraced half-sister to useful hurdler Balapour, runner-up in a County Hurdle. ***Lucinda Russell***

Conclusion: ***Winning pointer who fell at the last when all set to win on his second start over hurdles; very much a chasing type on looks***

Kieran Clark (Big John Wayne): *"Having seen plenty of the northern jumps scene in the winter months of last season, I'm expecting Lucinda Russell to have a fruitful 2024/25 with her novice chasers. Numerous horses from the yard appealed as types who would leave their form behind over fences and the one who caught my eye the most was Big John Wayne. He certainly lives up to his name in stature and would have got off the mark over hurdles at the second attempt but for falling at the last in a novice at Newcastle on Eider Chase day. An Irish point winner, Big John Wayne should thrive for the switch to chasing and, given his strong-galloping nature, looks a stayer to follow."*

Both Barrels h114

6 ch.g. Saddler's Rock (Ire) – Red Legend (Midnight Legend)
2023/24 h20s^{4} h22s^{3} h20.5v^{2} h22.7d* Apr 15

Local jockey Craig Nichol has ridden more winners at Kelso than any other track and he gained much his most valuable success in the saddle at that course in March when the Ewan Whillans-trained Cracking Rhapsody won the Morebattle Hurdle with its first prize of more than £60,000. Back at Kelso the following month, Nichol rode a double, partnering Cracking Rhapsody's stablemate Kingston Bridge in one of the finals of the Go North Series after landing another handicap hurdle earlier on the card with the progressive Both Barrels for Ewan Whillans' uncle Donald, both of whom train at nearby Hawick.

That was Both Barrels' first success and it certainly wasn't undeserved as he's yet to finish out of the frame in his seven outings. Starting off the previous season in bumpers, he belied his odds of 66/1 when running his best race on his third and final outing in that sphere to finish third behind another of our *Fifty*, Bertie's Ballet, in another of the Go North Finals at Kelso. Both Barrels made his hurdling debut in a novice at Carlisle last November, finishing fourth behind the useful Johnnywho who spent the rest of the season in graded company, and was then gambled on when third behind Worcester winner Ikarak in a similar event at Newcastle.

But Both Barrels found life a bit easier in handicaps and he showed improvement at Ayr in February. His jumping could have been a lot tidier, but he did well to see off all his rivals bar the easy winner Eire Street who turned out to be very well in under his penalty for winning at Carlisle the previous week. Both Barrels' first win was only delayed though, and off the same mark at Kelso he was able to go one better when sent off favourite to beat a largely exposed bunch. Staying on to lead approaching the last, he wasn't fluent at that flight but was ridden out to beat one of the outsiders, Bushypark, by two and a quarter lengths. The Kelso race, at just over two and three-quarter miles, was the furthest distance Both Barrels has raced over so far and he promises to stay three miles, being by high-class Flat stayer Saddler's Rock. ***Donald Whillans***

Conclusion: *Consistent type who got off the mark at Kelso on his final start and remains unexposed; a step up to three miles promises to suit*

Bucksy des Epeires (Fr) h121

5 b.g. Buck's Boum (Fr) – Maline des Epeires (Fr) (Ballingarry (Ire))

2023/24 h19.5d* h16v^{2} h20v^{4} h19.5d^{F} h19.3d h21.2s^{2} Apr 2

After an encouraging first season over hurdles for Venetia Williams following his purchase from France, Bucksy des Epeires looks set to embark on a successful career over fences this term in keeping with many from his stable before him. He was lightly raced in France where he wore a tongue tie for all his starts as well as a hood on his debut, finishing second on both his completed starts when trained by Donatien Sourdeau de Beauregard. That left him eligible for novices in Britain and he got off the mark at the first time of asking for his new stable, in a maiden at Lingfield in November, despite being off the track for more than a year beforehand. After travelling well, he kept on to lead in the final 100 yards and just held on by a nose from Dan Skelton's odds-on favourite Illico de Cotte with the pair of them finishing ten lengths clear.

Bucksy des Epeires progressed again when making his handicap debut in a valuable two-mile contest at Sandown on Tingle Creek day. The presence of Langer Dan at the top of the weights resulted in Bucksy des Epeires being 3 lb out of the handicap, though that was offset by conditional Ned Fox taking 5 lb off his back. Given that he was ridden more prominently than most, Bucksy des Epeires deserved credit for sustaining his effort as well as he did in the testing conditions, keeping on to finish three and a half lengths second to the useful Spirit d'Aunou. For the remainder of the season he was returned to longer trips, though it wasn't until his final outing at Ludlow in April that he showed something like his Sandown form after lesser efforts at Aintree and Ascot and a first-flight fall at Lingfield in between. At Ludlow, though, he got back on track, closing all the way to the line to be beaten a neck by outsider Legionar who held on to make all.

Bucksy des Epeires is by Buck's Boum, a half-brother to Big Buck's and best known now for siring dual Gold Cup winner Al Boum Photo, while his dam Maline des Epeires won all five of her starts in France, including three chases at Auteuil, showing useful form. A lengthy, angular gelding, Bucksy des Epeires could well prove just as good himself over fences. ***Venetia Williams***

Conclusion: ***Looks typical of the French imports who have been successful for his stable in the past and seems set to do well over fences***

Simon Walker (Bucksy des Epeires): *"Venetia Williams' French imports usually take time to find their feet in Britain, but when they hit the ground running it's time to sit up and take note. Bucksy des Epeires did just that last season and, though he didn't quite kick on in the expected manner, there's a strong chance he will in his second season, especially as he's very much bred to be a chaser, just the type his yard will progress through the ranks once the ground has eased."*

Caldwell Potter (Fr) h147p

6 gr.g. Martaline – Matnie (Fr) (Laveron)
2023/24 h16.5s² h16v* h16v* Dec 27

The record for the most expensive jumps horse sold at public auction was broken in the latest season when Caldwell Potter fetched €740,000 at Andy and Gemma Brown's dispersal at Tattersalls Ireland in February. That status proved relatively short-lived (when accounting for exchange rates) as Regent's Stroll set a new benchmark of £660,000 in July, but it was little surprise that Caldwell Potter had briefly raised the bar as rarely does a horse of his profile become available on the open market

Not only had he won a Grade 1 on his previous outing, but Caldwell Potter was also Timeform's second highest-rated novice hurdler at the time of sale (behind only Ballyburn) and comes from one of jump racing's most successful families being a brother of the ill-fated four-time Grade 1 winner Mighty Potter and a half-brother of rising star Brighterdaysahead, who has since won a Grade 1. His half-brothers French Dynamite and Indiana Jones have been successful at Grade 3 level.

There was a protracted battle in the sales ring between Gordon Elliott, who had trained the horse to win the Future Champions Novice Hurdle on his previous outing, and bloodstock agent Anthony Bromley, and it was the latter who prevailed. It was soon revealed that Caldwell Potter had been bought on behalf of John Hales, Ged Mason, Sir Alex Ferguson and Peter Done and would be sent to Paul Nicholls. Nicholls quickly ruled out a trip to the Cheltenham Festival with Caldwell Potter, stating that the horse would need more time to get acclimatised, but the record purchase was declared for the Mersey Novices' Hurdle at Aintree for a clash with his former stablemate and half-sister Brighterdaysahead. Sadly, an infected foot meant Caldwell Potter had to miss that engagement and we never got to see the extent of his ability over hurdles, but the form he showed when winning his Grade 1 at Leopardstown marks him out as one of the most exciting prospects for novice chases this season.

The Future Champions Novice Hurdle was run at a strong gallop on very testing ground and the test proved too much for most of the field, but Caldwell Potter was suited by such an emphasis being placed on stamina and he stuck to his task well to beat Predators Gold by six and a half lengths with a 38-length gap back to the third. Caldwell Potter, a decisive winner on two of his three starts over hurdles, has raced only at trips around two miles but will have no problem staying two and a half miles. ***Paul Nicholls***

Conclusion: *Grade 1-winning novice hurdler who comes from a superb jumping family; expected to take high rank in novice chase division for new yard*

Cuthbert Dibble (Ire) h137

6 b.g. Kayf Tara – Molo (Kalanisi (Ire))

2023/24 h19.5v* h24.3v* h24s^{3} h24.7d Apr 13

Cuthbert Dibble looked like a smart prospect for novice chasing last season but a setback, described by trainer Nigel Twiston-Davies as "a few muscle problems", meant that he didn't make his reappearance until the end of January and plans to go over fences were put on hold.

Cuthbert Dibble may have missed the first half of the season but he still enjoyed a productive campaign. He underlined his effectiveness on testing ground when drawing clear for a wide-margin win on his return in a two-and-a-half-mile handicap hurdle at Chepstow and then justified good support in a three-mile Pertemps qualifier at Haydock, winning with more in hand than the half-length margin might suggest after being closed down late on. That earned Cuthbert Dibble a crack at the series final at the Cheltenham Festival and he ran another fine race in third, seeing things out thoroughly and enhancing his reputation as a progressive and likeable hurdler. He was then down the field at Aintree, running his first disappointing race over hurdles, but it's easy enough to overlook that effort as he may still have been feeling the effects of his big effort in the Pertemps, while the drying ground possibly counted against him.

The tall, useful-looking Cuthbert Dibble has the physical stature to take well to chasing, while his consistent, progressive profile also bodes well for his prospects. He's a strong stayer and goes particularly well on testing ground so should be in for another productive winter, either in graded novices or valuable handicaps. ***Nigel Twiston-Davies***

Cuthbert Dibble appeals as one who should take well to chasing

Conclusion: *Progressed well over hurdles during a truncated campaign last season and has the tools to develop into a smart novice chaser; goes well when the mud is flying*

Demnat (Fr) c128

7 b.g. Doctor Dino (Fr) – Sandside (Fr) (Marchand de Sable (USA))

2023/24 c20s* c16.4s^{3} c26s c25s^{pu} Apr 13

French recruit Demnat had a 32-month absence to overcome when making his first start for Venetia Williams in a two-and-a-half-mile handicap chase at Ludlow in February but he did so in style, looking potentially smart as he travelled with enthusiasm on the front end before drawing 15 lengths clear. That was the clear highlight of the campaign for Demnat who was ultimately beaten a long way on two of his three subsequent starts and pulled up on the other occasion, but he shaped better than the result a couple of times and will be one to watch out for on his return after receiving some respite from the handicapper.

On his second start for the stable, and off a 10 lb higher mark than at Ludlow a few weeks earlier, Demnat dropped in trip to contest a handicap chase over an extended two miles at Newbury. He was no match for the impressive winner I'd Like To Know, who went on to win off a 14 lb higher mark at Kempton, but he was only a couple of lengths down on the runner-up until slithering on landing at the final fence and losing all momentum.

Two weeks later Demnat was then upped markedly in trip in the Fulke Walwyn Kim Muir Handicap Chase over three and a quarter miles at the Cheltenham Festival. He was only ninth but had jumped the third last in the lead and patently failed to stay in a strongly-run race on testing ground. Perhaps that run took something out of Denmat as he shaped as if amiss when pulled up at Aintree a month later, but he remains capable of bouncing back granted a summer break.

He's already shown his effectiveness when fresh and represents a trainer who excels with such types. Indeed, last season Williams' record with chasers running for the first time after an absence of 150 days or longer was 15 winners from 53 runners at a strike rate in excess of 28%, which returned a profit of £31 to £1 level stakes. Demnat is now only 5 lb higher in the weights than when successful at Ludlow, and if he is kept to trips at around two and a half miles it is expected that he will hold his form better. ***Venetia Williams***

Conclusion: *Looked potentially smart when overcoming a long layoff at Ludlow and had excuses afterwards; back on a handy mark and should be suited by the return to an intermediate trip*

Diamond Ri (Ire) — h123

5 ch.g. Diamond Boy (Fr) – Quaspia (Fr) (Fragrant Mix (Ire))

2023/24 h16.7s^2 h19s* h19.6v^4 h20.3g^2 Apr 17

Diamond Ri still looked fairly rough around the edges during a promising hurdling campaign but he's expected to sparkle over fences.

Diamond Ri was sent off a short-price favourite on his hurdling debut at Exeter in November having run out a wide-margin winner on his only start in bumpers the previous season, but, after looking like a big threat, his lack of experience seemed to tell in the home straight and he had to settle for an encouraging second. There was also an element of rawness about his display when getting off the mark over hurdles at Warwick on his next outing as he wasn't always fluent and looked a bit idle in front, but the way he had tanked into the lead on the turn for home was deeply impressive and marked him out as a good long-term prospect.

In the short-term, however, he found a step up in class in the listed Sidney Banks Memorial Novices' Hurdle coming too soon in his development and he didn't jump well enough to cope with the stiffer assignment, ultimately trailing home last of four and underlining that he was by no means the finished article. His season ended on a more positive note, however, as he was a good second in a two-and-a-half-mile novice hurdle at Cheltenham ten weeks later. Diamond Ri, making his first start away from testing ground, didn't have the pace to match the odds-on favourite Peaky Boy, who had been a good winner over course and distance on his only previous start over hurdles, but he stuck to his task in pleasing fashion up the run-in.

A half-brother to the very smart chaser Pencilfulloflead, Diamond Ri also appeals as one who will come into his own over fences. Inexperience held him back to an extent over hurdles but he should be a more mature model this time around and he has the raw materials to develop into a useful chaser. ***Joe Tizzard***

Conclusion: *Showed ability over hurdles despite looking far from the finished article; has a good jumping pedigree and will make a chaser*

Diva Luna (Ire) b109

5 b.m. Diamond Boy (Fr) – Longhouse Presents (Presenting)
2023/24 b16.6s* b17s* Apr 11

Ben Pauling had 11 runners in bumpers in the first two months of the year and seven of them won, four of those making winning debuts. The pick of them proved to be the mare Diva Luna who was pitched straight into a listed contest for her racecourse debut.

Five of her six rivals in the listed Alan Swinbank Mares' Bumper at Market Rasen were winners already, including favourite Park Princess, who had been an impressive ten-length winner on her debut at Newbury, and Avakate, who carried a penalty for winning a similar event at Doncaster, but Diva Luna proved well up to the task. She was allowed the run of things in front under a well-judged ride by Brian Hughes but still impressed with the way she readily quickened clear over two furlongs out. With her advantage reduced only late on, she had three-quarters of a length to spare at the line over the Dan Skelton-trained Listentoyourheart who had been runner-up to Avakate at Doncaster.

The previous season's Alan Swinbank winner Dysart Enos followed up in the Grade 2 Nickel Coin Mares' Bumper at Aintree and Diva Luna completed the same double just over two months later. It was a typically competitive renewal of the season's top bumper for mares, with all bar three of the 16 runners being winners and five of them having unbeaten records, but Diva Luna came out on top in similar fashion to her debut, this time with Kielan Woods doing the steering. Travelling well in the lead, Diva Luna responded generously when shaken up and was firmly in command at the line with three and a half lengths to spare over Paul Nicholls' Wincanton winner Jubilee Alpha.

Bought as a three-year-old for €50,000, the well-made Diva Luna had finished runner-up on her sole start in Irish points to Honky Tonk Highway who was in opposition at Aintree but finished down the field. Diva Luna is bred to stay well as her fairly useful half-sister Della Casa Lunga won at up to three miles over hurdles last season and her dam is a half-sister to the one-time smart Irish staying chaser Longhouse Poet. ***Ben Pauling***

Conclusion: *Made all to win both her bumpers, notably the Grade 2 mares' contest at Aintree, and looks a smart prospect for novice hurdles over further than two miles*

Doyen Quest (Ire) h122

6 ch.g. Doyen (Ire) – Queen of Questions (Ire) (Bob Back (USA))

23/24 b15.8d* b16.4v h16.7v^6 h19.5v^3 h16.5s* h16.5s^2 h16.3d* h20.3g* Apr 17

Doyen Quest's only outing in a point had been an eventful affair as the saddle slipped and his rider was unseated on the run-in when looking a certain winner, but his debut under Rules in a Ffos Las bumper in October went a lot smoother. Doyen Quest could be seen going notably well from a long way out at Ffos Las and, with no tack issues hindering him on this occasion, he scored in ready fashion to make the perfect start for Dan Skelton.

That win earned him a crack at a better bumper at Cheltenham the following month but he was made to look short of pace in that listed contest, finishing well held, and soon had his attentions switched to hurdles. It took Doyen Quest a bit of time to find his feet over hurdles as he didn't show a great deal on his debut at Exeter but he fared better when third at Chepstow next time and then took a bigger step forward to get off the mark in a maiden at Taunton in February. Even then he still looked a bit rough around the edges, but he was well on top at the finish, more so than the half-length margin would suggest. Back over the same course and distance the following month and making his handicap debut, Doyen Quest improved a bit more, finishing a length second to a generally progressive rival in Tintintin whilst pulling clear of the remainder.

But Doyen Quest ended a very successful first season winning a couple more handicaps at a time of year when his stable was going all out in the trainers' championship. Eleven days after Taunton, he was turned out at Newbury and narrowly went one better off the same mark, responding generously to get the better of useful novice Steel Ally by a neck with the remainder well strung out. There was a much more bunched finish when Doyen Quest followed up at Cheltenham in April but unexposed sorts mainly came to the fore in a competitive contest where he showed a really determined attitude to prevail by half a length from Whatsupwithyou. He's a lengthy sort with the scope to take to chasing but is open to further progress in handicap hurdles first. ***Dan Skelton***

Conclusion: *Enjoyed a productive campaign over hurdles and showed a good attitude to win his last couple of starts; should take well to chasing when the time comes*

Dysart Enos (Ire) h135p

6 b.m. Malinas (Ger) – Graces Benefit (Ire) (Beneficial)
2023/24 h15.8d* h16.8d* h16.6d* Jan 28

Looking on the bright side, Dysart Enos maintained her unbeaten record last term and added three wins over hurdles to the trio of victories she had notched in bumpers the previous season. She very much remains a mare to follow but connections had to suffer the disappointment of Dysart Enos having to miss what had been her big target all year, the Dawn Run Mares' Novices' Hurdle, at the eleventh hour. Fergal O'Brien reported that her overreach—when a horse strikes into one of its forelegs with a hind foot—wasn't a serious injury but the timing couldn't have been worse. No doubt some salt was rubbed into the wound by the result of the Dawn Run as the winner, Golden Ace, had finished nine lengths behind Dysart Enos when chasing her home in the Nickel Coin Mares' Bumper at Aintree the previous spring.

Dysart Enos had been the leading British-trained contender for the Dawn Run and her trainer's best chance of breaking his Festival duck. But she did win at her local track earlier in the season, landing the odds in a qualifier for the EBF 'National Hunt' series at Cheltenham's December meeting. She won it with authority, too, showing useful form and running to a level that would have made her competitive in graded company. Taking a keen hold in touch, Dysart Enos made smooth headway to lead entering the straight and kept on well for a ready two and three-quarter-length success over Beat The Bat with a big break to the rest.

That was much the best of her three wins over hurdles as Dysart Enos landed still shorter odds for her two other successes. Despite her jumping not being especially fluent, she had had little difficulty making a winning debut over hurdles against other mares in a novice at Huntingdon in November and she was found an excellent opportunity to complete her Festival preparations at Doncaster in January when easing clear without having to run anywhere near her Cheltenham form. Without that run at the Festival, her hurdling campaign arguably had more style than substance, though the same can't be said of her bumper win at Aintree which has thrown up plenty of winners over hurdles besides Golden Ace. The listed mares' hurdle on Charlie Hall day at Wetherby has been pencilled in for her return. ***Fergal O'Brien***

Conclusion: *Unbeaten mare who is likely to remain a formidable opponent against her own sex; has yet to show everything she has to offer*

Gentle Slopes **h126p**

7 b.g. Gentlewave (Ire) – Dalriath (Fraam)

2023/24 h16d* Jan 13

Hopefully the gentle approach taken with Gentle Slopes will pay off. A listed bumper winner for Milton Harris, he has raced only once since joining Nicky Henderson during the latest jumps season, but his victory in a two-mile novice hurdle at Kempton marked him down as one to keep on the right side.

Gentle Slopes was all out—and had to survive a stewards' inquiry—to land the odds on his stable debut in January, but there was a lot to like about the way he knuckled down on his first start for more than a year to beat a couple of fairly useful rivals who both won next time. That effort can also be upgraded slightly as Gentle Slopes had to work hard to see off the eventual third on the run to the final flight and then had to dig deep again to deny his final challenger by a nose.

Gentle Slopes had been disappointing in a two-and-a-half-mile maiden hurdle at Cheltenham on his final start for Harris, though he had shaped well when third in a good-quality novice on his hurdling debut at the same track. He was also successful

Gentle Slopes (right) was a narrow winner at Kempton on his first start for Nicky Henderson

on two of his three starts in bumpers, including a listed event at Cheltenham, and his profile is largely positive. An opening handicap mark of 121 may prove tempting for connections, though his good jumping pedigree and background (was a wide-margin winner of an Irish point) suggest that he should make up into a useful novice chaser. Either way, he remains with untapped potential after only one start for his leading yard. ***Nicky Henderson***

Conclusion: *Dug deep to make a winning start for his new stable and should still have more to offer; has the makings of a talented novice chaser*

Gidleigh Park h138

6 b.g. Walk In The Park (Ire) – Lindeman (Ire) (Presenting)
2023/24 h16.7s* h20.5v* h20.3d* h24v^{6} Mar 15

A total of just nine British-trained runners contested the three Irish-dominated novice hurdles at the Cheltenham Festival. According to the betting, the best chance of one of those being kept at home was the Albert Bartlett in which Harry Fry's unbeaten Gidleigh Park started the 9/2 second favourite. It turned out, though, that the longest priced of the four British-trained runners, Ben Pauling's The Jukebox Man, went much the closest after being caught in the dying strides by the Gordon Elliott-trained outsider Stellar Story. As for Gidleigh Park, he could make no impression back in sixth after not settling fully on a first try at three miles. But he was the pick of the Albert Bartlett field on looks beforehand, being a tall, chasing type, and he remains an exciting novice chase prospect.

Gidleigh Park had won all four of his starts up until the Festival, beginning with a bumper at Chepstow the previous spring in which he'd had The Jukebox Man six lengths back in second. Starting off over hurdles over two miles, he landed short odds at Exeter in November and followed up impressively a month later in an EBF qualifier at Newbury over another half-mile, leading on the bridle two out and quickening clear on the run-in to beat Paul Nicholls' Fire Flyer, winner of his next two starts, by nine lengths.

That earned Gidleigh Park a rise in class and he was sent off the 5/6 favourite against five other unexposed rivals in the Grade 2 novice on Cheltenham's Trials Day in January. He did a lot wrong in a muddling race, refusing to settle in the lead, but showed a willing attitude to regain his advantage after being headed before the final flight and got the better of Lucky Place, who was later a good fourth in the Coral Cup, by half a length.

Like another of our *Fifty*, Regent's Stroll, Gidleigh Park is from the family of Denman. Gidleigh Park's dam Lindeman, winner of a mares' bumper at Cheltenham and a maiden hurdle at Warwick, is out of a half-sister to the 2008 Gold Cup winner. Gidleigh Park is a half-brother to a couple of winners, G A Henty and St Barts, who stay three miles or thereabouts, but he is likely to be campaigned over shorter distances. ***Harry Fry***

Conclusion: ***Lost his unbeaten record at the Cheltenham Festival when proving too free on a first try at three miles, but stood out on looks beforehand and remains an exciting novice chase prospect***

Good And Clever (Ire) b110

5 br.g. Soldier of Fortune (Ire) – Grangeclare Rosa (Ire) (Gamut (Ire))
2023/24 b16v* b17d^3 Apr 13

Soldier of Fortune routed his field in a soft-ground Irish Derby in 2007, powering clear to win by nine lengths, and his son Good And Clever showed that testing going won't be an issue when running out a wide-margin winner at Warwick under even more gruelling conditions which were too much for most of his young rivals to cope with. Sent off at 8/1 for his debut, Good And Clever travelled fluently before improving to lead early in the straight and then forged clear to win by a dozen lengths from the favourite Les's Destiny Star who was penalised for his win at Doncaster. Most of the rest finished at wide intervals, with even the fifth horse beaten more than 40 lengths.

Wide-margin bumper winners in the mud are often difficult to assess but Good And Clever showed he didn't need bad ground to be at his best when displaying much-improved form on no worse than good to soft going at Aintree the following month. With the Champion Bumper at Cheltenham often dominated by Irish stables nowadays, Aintree's Grade 2 bumper which rounds off Grand National day has become something of an alternative championship for British-trained bumper horses. The latest renewal was dominated by Fergal O'Brien who trained the first two home, Horaces Pearl and Tripoli Flyer, the latter another member of our *Fifty*, and Good And Clever took a big step forward from his Warwick win to take third behind them. Leading for the first couple of furlongs and then again briefly early in the straight, Good And Clever kept on to be beaten just over two lengths behind the winner.

Good And Clever was a €40,000 purchase by his trainer as a three-year-old. Not even Willie Mullins could conjure a win out of his dam Grangeclare Rosa under Rules, though she was placed several times in bumpers and in hurdles at up to three miles. She did win a point, though, and is a half-sister to several winning jumpers, including the useful pair Grangeclare Lark and Scarthy Lad, the latter successful over both hurdles and fences. Good And Clever is likely to be suited by further than two miles once he goes over hurdles. ***Warren Greatrex***

Conclusion: ***Won a Warwick bumper on bottomless going on his debut but also ran well under less testing conditions at Aintree; promises to stay quite well in novice hurdles***

Goshhowposh (Ire) h126p

7 b.g. Malinas (Ger) – Keelans Choice (Ire) (Croco Rouge (Ire))
2023/24 h23.1s* h24.3d^{ur} h24.7s* h23.1v^{pu} h24.3d^{6} Mar 30

Goshhowposh looks a thorough stayer, as is typical of horses by Malinas, the likes of Mister Malarky and Broadway Boy examples of that, and there will be more opportunities to have those stamina reserves tested when he goes chasing this season.

Options are limited for a staying hurdler of a certain standard but Philip Hobbs and Johnson White got a year's worth of experience into Goshhowposh in three-mile handicaps last season, targeting a Pertemps qualifier at Wincanton on Boxing Day, which he won with ease and looked better the further he went, before he was pulled up in another qualifier in the same series on heavy ground at Exeter in February.

That ended any hopes of making the cut for the Final itself at the Cheltenham Festival in March, but he got back on track, despite finishing only sixth, at Haydock on his final start of the campaign. Goshhowposh went with more zest in first-time blinkers, looking like the progressive novice he'd seemed prior to Exeter, and he was contesting the lead when making a bad mistake two out that probably cost him a place.

Careless jumping had also hindered him on his first couple of starts of the season and resulted in an unseating at Haydock in November, but prior to that he had overcome mistakes to win on his return at Exeter where he gamely stuck to his task and looked to have bags of stamina. He'll need to jump better over fences but his stamina and effectiveness on testing ground—both of his wins came on ground described as soft by Timeform—will give connections plenty of options this winter and he appeals as one who still has more to offer. ***Philip Hobbs & Johnson White***

Conclusion: *Stiffer tests in long-distance chases could bring out the best in this lightly-raced stayer*

Grey Dawning (Ire) c160

7 gr.g. Flemensfirth (USA) – Lady Wagtail (Ire) (Milan)
2023/24 c24.2s^{3} c21.6d* c20.6d^{2} c24s* c19.8s* c19.9s^{3} Apr 11

It was a Cheltenham Festival to remember for Dan Skelton whose four winners included a Grade 1 double on the third day of the meeting, kicked off by Grey Dawning's gritty victory in the Turners Novices' Chase. The Irish had been responsible for the first three home in the Arkle and the first two in the Brown Advisory, but it was a different story in the Turners as Britain's top two novice chasers, Grey Dawning and Ginny's Destiny, effectively had the race to themselves as they turned into the straight.

Grey Dawning had finished runner-up to Ginny's Destiny when the pair clashed in a novice chase at Cheltenham in December but he was giving the winner 3 lb on

Grey Dawning puts in a stunning leap to seal the Turners Novices' Chase

that occasion and, more importantly, had made a shocking mistake at the second last when looming up. Grey Dawning is essentially a fluent jumper, though, and in the Turners he put in a superb round which helped him to reverse the placings with his old rival and score by a couple of lengths, with the runner-up eight lengths clear of another British-trained contender, Djelo, in third.

Ginny's Destiny was a place in advance of Grey Dawning when they clashed again at Aintree in the Manifesto Novices' Chase but both had to settle for minor honours behind Arkle third Il Etait Temps whose speed proved decisive in a race run at a stop-start gallop that placed far less emphasis on stamina than had been the case in the Turners which was run at a strong tempo throughout. It's also possible that the ding-dong battle at Cheltenham had taken the edge off Ginny's Destiny and Grey Dawning at Aintree, and they are better judged on the form they had shown in the Turners.

Grey Dawning had announced himself as a big player in the novice chase division with an emphatic nine-and-a-half-length success in the graduation chase on Haydock's Betfair Chase card. He appeals as a leading contender for the main event this time around as he seems likely to be suited by the return to three miles given how thoroughly he saw out the trip when successful in a well-run edition of the Hampton Novices' Chase at Warwick in January. ***Dan Skelton***

Conclusion: *Produced high-class effort to win at the Cheltenham Festival and establish himself as Britain's top novice chaser; unexposed as a stayer and can make his mark in open Grade 1s*

Imperial Saint (Fr) h124

6 b.g. Saint des Saints (Fr) – Quinine de Mazille (Fr) (Network (Ger))
2023/24 h15.8s* h16s^{2} h16.3d^{3} h18.5v^{3} h20d* Apr 22

Four-time Champion Jockey Richard Johnson will forever be remembered for his fruitful partnership with Philip Hobbs and particularly the high-profile horses they teamed up with like 2003 Champion Hurdle winner Rooster Booster. Since retiring in 2021, Johnson has started a couple of ownership syndicates and he has struck lucky with the two horses he bought at the Goffs UK Spring Sale in May 2023 as both Imperial Saint and Party Vibes have made bright starts and feature among our *Fifty* to follow.

Imperial Saint was bought for £40,000 after decisively winning a Toomebridge point on his third go in that sphere around a fortnight before his sale, and it soon proved to be money well spent as he got off the mark on his debut under Rules at Ludlow in November in the family colours Johnson had worn when riding his first winner in 1994. Sent off at 13/2 for a two-mile maiden hurdle, Imperial Saint made most of the running and, despite running green in stages, was an emphatic nine-and-a-half length winner under Micheal Nolan. He had to settle for minor honours on his next three outings, but he raised his game on his final start of the season to win a Ffos Las handicap on his first attempt at two and a half miles.

The way Imperial Saint hangs to his left is starting to look like an ingrained trait and is a slight concern, but it didn't stop him forging clear at Ffos Las and it's worth focusing on how that step up in trip triggered a bigger effort. He remains completely unexposed at intermediate trips and is likely to do better, particularly when going over fences given his pointing background and his sire Saint des Saints' record as a rich source of quality steeplechasers. ***Philip Hobbs & Johnson White***

Conclusion: *Produced his best effort yet when upped in trip at Ffos Las on his final start of the campaign; still unexposed over intermediate trips and should do well over fences*

Inthewaterside (Fr) h131

6 b.g. Jeu St Eloi (Fr) – Vared (Fr) (Denham Red (Fr))
2023/24 h20s* h15.7g^{4} h19.5d* h19.3d^{2} h20s^{3} Apr 12

Paul Nicholls has a host of promising youngsters going chasing this season—four of them are included in our *Fifty*—but perhaps the one who will benefit most from the switch to fences is the imposing Inthewaterside. Dual bumper winner Inthewaterside also won a couple of times over hurdles last season, showing useful form in the process, but it's as a staying chaser that he is expected to thrive and make the step up to graded company.

Inthewaterside made heavy weather of landing the odds in a steadily run two-and-a-half-mile maiden hurdle at Aintree and then proved short of pace when last of four in an introductory hurdle over two miles at Ascot. That represented a rather underwhelming start for a horse who had shown so much promise in bumpers, but he got back on track when faced with a greater emphasis on stamina on his final three starts of the campaign at around two and a half miles. The most impressive aspect of his victory on his handicap hurdle debut at Lingfield in January was how he found plenty to fend off a late challenger, and that response to pressure was also evident when third in a competitive handicap hurdle at Aintree on his final outing. Inthewaterside forced a strong gallop at Aintree, and wasn't helped by some inconsistent jumping, but he enhanced his reputation by staying in the fight for so long, only cracking inside the final 100 yards.

The concern with Inthewaterside is that he got very worked up when runner-up to Pic Roc in an Ascot novice, and he was also on his toes ahead of his final start at Aintree when wearing a hood for the first time, but he's entitled to mature with experience and is in excellent hands to fulfil his potential. His response to pressure suggests that the step up to three miles, as well as the switch to chasing, can be a catalyst for improvement. ***Paul Nicholls***

Conclusion: *Imposing sort who showed useful form over hurdles but can raise his game further over fences*

Into The Park (Ire) h129

5 b.g. Walk In The Park (Ire) – La Sarrazine (Fr) (Medicean)
2023/24 b16.3s h17v^{ur} h16.5d^{3} h16.3s* h16.5s* h18.8d^{4} Mar 23

Philip Hobbs first won the Greatwood Hurdle at Cheltenham in 2002 with Rooster Booster who put up a top-class performance, one which he was to repeat in the Champion Hurdle back at Cheltenham the following spring. Hobbs has won the Greatwood another three times since with Detroit City, Menorah and Garde La Victoire who were all at least smart over hurdles, as was Gumball who went very close to giving the stable another win in the race in 2019. Into The Park isn't that good yet, but he's unexposed and might be the type to creep into the race on a handy weight.

The well-made Into The Park takes a very positive profile into his second season over hurdles. A faller on his only start in Irish points, he began last season in a bumper at Newbury and even though he was beaten a long way he showed signs of ability as well as inexperience. Switched to hurdles at Aintree a month later, he was in the process of showing a bit more when stumbling and unseating before three out. But his next outing in a maiden hurdle at Taunton revealed much more of his ability as he stayed on to finish a close third behind the well-regarded pair, Joyeuse and Tutti

Quanti, trained by Nicky Henderson and Paul Nicholls respectively. There was more quantity than quality in the similar event that Into The Park contested at Newbury later in January but he won it readily by eight lengths after travelling well in the lead.

A BHA mark of 120 looked quite a lenient one given the ease of that success and, sent off as the 6/5 favourite, he duly followed up on his handicap debut back at Taunton in February. Leading when hanging left approaching the last, he was driven clear for a three-length win over another last-time-out winner, Inca de Lafayette, trained by Nicholls. His bid for a hat-trick in a novices' handicap at Newbury in March was unsuccessful, even though the slightly longer trip had been expected to suit, but he wasn't disgraced in fourth behind Irish raider I Love My Baie and still looks one to keep on side. ***Philip Hobbs & Johnson White***

Conclusion: *Failed in his hat-trick bid on his final start but had been going the right way prior to that and remains unexposed as a handicap hurdler*

Dan Barber (Into The Park): *"There's hope courtesy a clutch of youngsters that it will be a productive campaign out of Minehead this season and the handicapper with perhaps the most scope for improvement among them is Into The Park, whose absence since a closing third at Newbury perhaps suggests he just wasn't himself there. His earlier back-to-back wins at two miles on sharp tracks read well, not least as he's surely going to prove best over longer trips."*

Iroko (Fr) c154p

6 b.g. Cokoriko (Fr) – Boscraie (Fr) (Martaline)

2023/24 c20v* c19.8s^5 c25s^2 Apr 12

Most horses arriving at the Cheltenham Festival do so at concert pitch given the meeting's importance in the jumps calendar, though that wasn't the case with Iroko when he lined up in the latest edition of the Turners Novices' Chase. That's no slight against Oliver Greenall and Josh Guerriero, who had primed him perfectly to win the Martin Pipe Conditional Jockeys' Handicap Hurdle at the meeting the previous season, but a reflection of the race against time the trainers faced with a horse who at one stage had been ruled out for the season.

Iroko had created an excellent impression when easily brushing aside some well-regarded rivals on his chasing debut at Warwick in November, but later that month it was reported he had picked up a foot injury and would be out of action for the rest of the campaign. He recovered faster than expected, though, to such an extent that he was able to take his chance in the Turners. In a race run at a strong gallop throughout, Iroko understandably looked rusty and was no threat from the top of the hill, though he plugged on in fifth and was by no means disgraced given the interrupted preparation and his lack of experience.

Iroko duly proved much sharper for that outing and also appreciated the step up in trip at Aintree's Grand National meeting where he showed form bordering on very smart to finish runner-up in the Grade 1 Mildmay Novices' Chase behind impressive Fulke Walwyn Kim Muir Handicap Chase winner Inothewayurthinkin. Iroko's only previous outing at around three miles was when third in the Grade 1 Sefton Novices' Hurdle at the 2023 Grand National meeting, so he remains with untapped potential as a stayer and appeals as one capable of raising his game given an injury-free campaign. The Coral Gold Cup would seem like a suitable early-season target for one with his profile.
Oliver Greenall & Josh Guerriero

Conclusion: *Suffered an injury-hit campaign but still marked himself out as a high-class prospect; unexposed as a staying chaser and remains likely to do better*

Jango Baie (Fr) h148p

5 b.g. Tiger Groom – Tenessee (Fr) (Kapgarde (Fr))
2023/24 h15.7d* h16.5v* h19.6v^2 h18.1s^2 h20s^2 Apr 12

As part of some major changes to the jumps programme, the Tolworth Novices' Hurdle was moved to form the centrepiece of Aintree's new Boxing Day card and was run as the Formby Novices' Hurdle. Nicky Henderson had a particularly good record in the Grade 1 when it was held at Sandown, winning it six times, most recently with Constitution Hill in 2022, and he took the first running at the race's new home with Jango Baie. The likely winner appeared to be the Gordon Elliott-trained favourite Farren Glory, who had won the Royal Bond at Fairyhouse earlier in the month, but he fell when going well in the lead two out and that left Jango Baie and Favour And Fortune to fight it out with the former finding plenty to draw two and three-quarter lengths clear.

Jango Baie was following up a narrow debut success over fellow *Fifty* member Tellherthename, who disappointed in the Formby, in an Ascot novice which Henderson had previously won with the likes of Altior and My Tent Or Yours. But Jango Baie didn't manage to add to those successes, and it wasn't it until he returned to Aintree in the spring that he fully restored his reputation. Before that he was twice a beaten favourite, going down to the unbeaten Handstands in the Sidney Banks Memorial Novices' Hurdle at Huntingdon and then coming out best at the weights again behind another Ben Pauling-trained winner when beaten half a length by Personal Ambition in the Premier Novices' Hurdle at Kelso.

Instead of one of the graded contests at Aintree, Jango Baie contested the two-and-a-half-mile premier handicap and ran his best race all season on Timeform's

Jango Baie was a huge eye-catcher at Aintree

figures with a most eye-catching run after things went against him in the straight. Losing momentum and carried left when one of the leaders unseated in front of him after the second last, Jango Baie was still only fourth jumping the final flight but finished strongly to be beaten a length and three-quarters behind one of the joint-favourites Kateira. That smart effort made him the highest-rated British-trained novice last season and identifies him as a fine prospect for novice chases. ***Nicky Henderson***

Conclusion: *Grade 1 novice hurdle winner who very much caught the eye when a strong-finishing second in a handicap back at Aintree; should be at least as good over fences*

Jurancon (Fr) b105

5 b.g. Free Port Lux – Bamos (Fr) (Coastal Path)

2023/24 b16v* b16.3s^2 b16.2s* Mar 27

You're not imagining things if you have a sense of déjà vu about a French-bred horse named Jurancon running for the Pipe yard. Going back 20 years or so, Jurancon II was a smart staying chaser trained by Martin Pipe for David Johnson. He finished third in the Midlands Grand National on just his second start over fences and the following season won two valuable handicaps, the Summer National back at Uttoxeter and the Grand

National Trial at Haydock. After running away with the latter contest by 15 lengths, he was sent off one of the 10/1 co-favourites for the 2004 Grand National under Sir Anthony McCoy but fell at the fourth.

The current Jurancon trained by David Pipe also looks destined for a successful jumping career at Pond House after winning two of his bumpers and finishing a good second in the other one. After easily winning the second of his two starts in Irish points, Jurancon made his debut at Chepstow in December and ran out a ready winner by eight lengths from another of our *Fifty*, Ski Lodge, who'd finished ahead of him when they made their point debuts in Ireland. Ski Lodge went one better back at Chepstow the following month, and while Jurancon was unable to follow up under a penalty at Newbury on his next start, he acquitted himself well in staying on for second, two and a half lengths behind Roysse from the Ben Pauling stable which was firing in bumper winners at that stage of the season. However, Jurancon ended his season on a winning note at Hereford in March. He and the other winner in the field, Rocking Man, who'd also made a winning debut at Chepstow, dominated the betting with Sam Thomas' charge sent off a shade of odds-on. However, in a well-run race by bumpers standards, Jurancon came out on top by three lengths after asserting in the last 100 yards.

A sturdy gelding but not yet the finished article, Jurancon is a half-brother to useful staying chaser Git Maker who was placed in the Kim Muir and Scottish Grand National in the spring for Jamie Snowden. That gives an indication of where Jurancon's longer-term future lies, but there are races to be won with him over hurdles first. ***David Pipe***

Conclusion: ***Winning pointer who's bred to stay well over fences in due course, so it's encouraging that he showed plenty in bumpers***

Kel du Large (Fr) h114p

4 b.g. No Risk At All (Fr) – Princesse Selenia (Fr) (Kapgarde (Fr))
2023/24 b13.2s* b14s* h16.2s* Feb 25

Jane Williams, a chartered accountant before training racehorses, describes her career change as being the result of 'a hobby gone wrong', but that's a tongue-in-cheek view of what has, in fact, been a success story for her Devon stable. Much of that success has been founded on a system of buying jumping-bred yearlings or two-year-olds from France for a fraction of the sums which change hands for Irish pointers, for example. The type of horse which the yard specialises in is much better catered for by the racing programme these days, following the recent introduction of juvenile hurdles restricted to National Hunt-bred horses, in addition to the more established junior bumpers.

Kel du Large exploited some of those opportunities to really good effect last season, winning all three of his starts. Although sent off at 16/1 for his debut in a junior bumper at Exeter in October, Kel du Large clearly knew his job well in a field of other newcomers as he made all the running, was in command over a furlong out and won by three lengths. That win meant that Kel du Large started joint favourite for the listed junior bumper on Cheltenham's New Year's Day card and he wasn't hard pressed to follow up. Getting a lead this time but travelling well close up, he went on with over half a mile to run and kept on well to beat Nigel Twiston-Davies' Huntingdon winner Dirty Den by two and three-quarter lengths. Those two bumper wins clearly made Kel du Large the one to beat on his debut over hurdles in a Junior 'National Hunt' Hurdle at Hereford in February and he duly landed the odds, making the running again and staying on well to beat the Jonjo O'Neill newcomer Don Virginia by two and a quarter lengths.

Bought for €33,000 as a two-year-old at Deauville, the sturdy Kel du Large is a half-brother to a couple of winning jumpers in France, while his unraced dam is a sister to Princesse Kap who was a smart chaser around Auteuil. He's also from the wider family of Queen Mother Champion Chase winner Politologue and dual Grand Steeple-Chase de Paris winner Docteur du Ballon. It's worth noting that Kel du Large will remain eligible for novice hurdles this season. ***Jane Williams***

Conclusion: *Unbeaten in two bumpers and a junior hurdle, laying a solid foundation for one with the profile to keep progressing for a while yet*

Lady In The Park (Ire) h109

6 b.m. Walk In The Park (Ire) – Emily's Flyer (Ire) (Oscar (Ire))

2023/24 b17s^3 h15.8v^3 h19.7v* h24.3v^2 h21.4g^2 h26.6s^5 Apr 25

With 37 winners last season, all bar five of which were provided by Lucinda Russell, Patrick Wadge was the champion conditional rider. The 22-year-old has been no overnight success as it took him more than 60 rides to achieve his first winner, which came for Russell at Perth in April 2022 after having his first ride under Rules at the same track in August 2020. But the winners have flowed much more regularly since, with Wadge enjoying a 20% strike-rate for his stable last season.

Among those winners was Lady In The Park who he was partnering for the first time when she won a mares' novice hurdle at Wetherby on Boxing Day. That was Lady In The Park's third start after she had shown promise to finish third in a bumper at Aintree and another mares' novice on her hurdling debut at Uttoxeter. Lady In The Park was suited by a step up in trip at Wetherby and proved a determined winner, challenging two out and then edging ahead close home to beat subsequent winner Dontyawantme by half a length. Even more of a test of stamina looked likely to suit Lady In The Park and she duly ran well next time when stepped up to three miles for her handicap debut at Ayr, keeping on to dead-heat for second three-quarters of a length behind winner Shoeshine Boy. Although beaten at odds-on next time in a mares' handicap at the same track, Lady In The Park ran well, especially considering the drop back in trip and much quicker conditions, giving plenty of weight to winner Donso Star. A steady pace had also counted against her there and it was a similar story on her final start at Perth where, under the circumstances, she ran creditably in fifth.

Lady In The Park, who was bought for £90,000 after winning her second start in Irish points, is a rangy mare who is built to make an even better chaser. Her dam Emily's Flyer was a fairly useful winner over hurdles at up to three miles for Fergal O'Brien and a half-sister to useful staying chaser Little Bruce and very smart mare Feathard Lady who won all her seven starts, notably the Christmas Hurdle. ***Lucinda Russell***

Conclusion: *Solid start over hurdles and looks the type to do better still over fences, especially as she remains unexposed over staying trips*

Le Fauve (Fr) h120

4 ch.g. Masterstroke (USA) – Grenadines Island (Fr) (Bonnet Rouge (Fr))
2023/24 h16.4s^{2} h17v^{3} h16.8d^{5} h16.3v^{2} Mar 1

Le Fauve's failure to win a race over hurdles so far, whilst frustrating on the face of it, might well prove to be a blessing in disguise. Had he won as a juvenile, it would have restricted his options this term but the fact that he remains eligible for novice contests should make him that much easier to place. Being a lengthy, useful-looking gelding, he also seems the type who'll need a bit more time to strengthen so another season as a novice certainly won't be lost on him.

Le Fauve, who was wearing a tongue tie, very nearly got off the mark at the first time of asking as he was touched off by a nose in a hurdle for unraced three-year-olds at Bordeaux for Joel Boisnard. The winner of that race, incidentally, Anzadam, looks a useful recruit for Willie Mullins and Joe and Marie Donnelly, as he went on to win his next start before his export to Ireland and was as short as 16/1 for the Triumph Hurdle last winter though has yet to make his debut for his new connections.

Anzadam was sold privately but Le Fauve joined Skelton for €105,000 after an online sale just ten days after his debut. Le Fauve was quite highly tried on his first start for new connections but was sent off the 5/2 favourite for a listed contest at Aintree in December. He shaped promisingly in finishing nine lengths third behind Paul Nicholls' Liari, briefly looking a bigger threat to the winner than eventual runner-up Knight of Allen. He faced a stiffer task next time when taking on the top juvenile hurdler Sir Gino in the Finesse Juvenile Hurdle on Cheltenham's Trials Day card in January and weakened to finish a well-held fifth of the seven runners but travelled well for a long way.

Le Fauve's final start, against four rivals in a more ordinary juvenile at Newbury at the beginning of March, looked much more winnable but he had to settle for second at a shade of odds-on, beaten four and a half lengths by Ithaca's Arrow in a race that didn't suit him tactically. Le Fauve has a couple of winning juvenile hurdlers in France among his siblings and, given both his physique and jumping pedigree, he shouldn't have any difficulty winning races this season. ***Dan Skelton***

Conclusion: *Showed promise without winning in his juvenile season when highly tried on occasions but could well be the type to flourish as he strengthens this term*

Lord of Thunder (Ire) h121p

6 br.g. Getaway (Ger) – Harbour Mistress (Ire) (Presenting)

2023/24 h19.5d^{pu} h21.4s^{2} h19.8v* h21.4v* Jan 6

The Persian War, run at Chepstow in October, was won in fine style last season by Champion Bumper third Captain Teague who dispatched a host of previous winners on his first start over hurdles. He wasn't the only hurdling debutant in the line-up, however, as among his rivals was Lord of Thunder, the 80/1 outsider of the seven who had finished third in a bumper at Stratford the previous spring when shaping with promise. The Persian War proved too stiff an introduction over hurdles for Lord of Thunder—he was pulled up—but he fared much better with his sights lowered to

Lord of Thunder pings a hurdle on his way to a comfortable victory at Wincanton

ordinary novice company, contesting three such races at Wincanton and winning the last two of them in the style of one to follow.

Still looking to have something to learn on his next start, he shaped encouragingly nonetheless in finishing runner-up to Captain Teague's stablemate Il Pino but soon went one better against another from the Nicholls yard, Tarras Wood, on his third start over hurdles in December. Lord of Thunder impressed in almost every respect in easily dismissing the other joint-favourite, jumping and travelling well and having his five remaining rivals well strung out at the finish in heavy ground. Less than three weeks later, Lord of Thunder followed up under a penalty in near-identical fashion and in similarly testing conditions. It was a slowly-run race but there was no mistaking Lord of Thunder's quality again as he travelled powerfully and quickened away between the last two hurdles.

Lord of Thunder looks likely to carry on improving and that progress may well come over fences as he was second on his only start in Irish points before being bought for £165,000. There are some good jumpers in his family, notably top-class chaser Harbour Pilot, his grandam's half-brother, who twice finished third behind Best Mate in the Cheltenham Gold Cup. ***Joe Tizzard***

Conclusion: *Highly tried on his hurdling debut but hard to fault when winning his last couple of starts in the mud at Wincanton in very good style*

Mahland (Ire) h115

6 ch.g. Mahler – Ebaniya (Ire) (Sinndar (Ire))

2023/24 h19.5s^5 h19s h23.8v^2 h21.6v^2 h23.9s* Apr 16

The best horse to have carried the yellow and green colours of Lady Dulverton is smart chaser Happygolucky, runner-up in the Ultima at the 2021 Cheltenham Festival before going one better in a Grade 3 handicap at Aintree. Trained by Kim Bailey, Happygolucky looked the type who'd stay long distances and the same owner's Mahland is another who should be well suited by longer trips once he goes over fences. He certainly improved last season over hurdles once his stamina began to be tested more fully and, being a strong, workmanlike type who has already won a point, he looks well up to winning chases under Rules.

Mahland won his point in the spring of 2023 over two and a half miles but that sort of trip proved inadequate for him on his first couple of runs over hurdles at Chepstow and Warwick. But he left those efforts well behind when stepped up to three miles for a maiden hurdle at Ludlow in February. Jumping well in the lead, Mahland relished the longer trip and rallied well in the closing stages after being headed two out to be beaten a length and a half by the favourite Monks Meadow. Mahland was runner-up again next time over a slightly shorter trip in a novices' handicap at Exeter, going down by half a length to Jupiter Allen after disputing the lead with that rival throughout on very testing ground which contributed to the other five runners all being pulled up. Back at three miles, Mahland justified favouritism on his final start in a handicap at Ffos Las in April. Progressing further, he again led or disputed throughout before asserting under hands and heels to win by four lengths from Minella Blueway. With the exception of his second start, Mahland was the subject of good support in each of his races.

By Mahler who's proving a good source of staying chasers, Mahland was a €38,000 purchase as a three-year-old and he comes from a very good Aga Khan family. Grandam Ebadiyla won the Irish Oaks and Prix Royal-Oak and the latest Oaks winner Ezeliya is from the same family too, but it has also produced some good jumpers, including his dam's half-brother Ebaziyan, winner of the Supreme Novices' for Willie Mullins in 2007. Raced only on soft or heavy going, Mahland is one to follow given a stamina test over fences. ***Mel Rowley***

Conclusion: ***Straightforward type who progressed over hurdles and is likely to do well given a good test of stamina over fences***

Monty Bodkin (Ire) b101

5 b.g. Walk In The Park (Ire) – La Segnora (Fr) (Turgeon (USA))
2023/24 b15.7d^{2} b17v^{6} b16.6v* Feb 21

Some of jumping's higher-profile owners re-evaluated their futures in the game last season and among them were Andrew and Jane Megson, long-time supporters of Ben Pauling's increasingly successful Cotswolds yard. The Megsons' association with Pauling brought them a Cheltenham Festival winner as recently as 2022 when Global Citizen won the Grand Annual but, explaining the couple's decision to reduce their string and move their remaining horses elsewhere, Andrew Megson said: 'The real driver is about making sure we enjoy it because it is a hobby and we don't want it to be a grind. So we decided to thin out and while we did that we took the opportunity to make a few changes.'

As a result, a handful of the Megsons' horses have now joined Jonjo and AJ O'Neill, including a couple of our *Fifty*, Monty Bodkin and Tellherthename. Monty Bodkin really impressed on looks last season, being a strong, attractive gelding, and showed plenty of ability to go with it in bumpers for his former stable. Despite signs of inexperience, he made a promising start to his career at Ascot in November when finishing four and a quarter lengths second to the favourite Celtic Dino, taking a keen hold but keeping on in the final furlong. Monty Bodkin initially failed to build on that promise when dropping away at Aintree on Boxing Day but his stable was having a quiet spell at that stage of the season. But it was firing on all cylinders again in the New Year when Monty

Bodkin made the expected progress from his debut at the second attempt, getting off the mark at Doncaster in February. Never far away and travelling well, he asserted approaching the final 100 yards and won with a bit more than his winning margin of a length and three-quarters implies from the penalised Fontwell winner Tom Doniphon with the pair pulling clear.

Bought for €105,000 as a three-year-old, Monty Bodkin is a brother to two winners under Rules, including fairly useful hurdler/chaser El Muchacho, while his year-younger brother No Drama This End has won his only start in points. Their dam La Segnora was a very good jumper in France where her eight wins included the Grade 1 Grand Prix d'Automne over hurdles and France's most valuable handicap chase, the Prix du President de la Republique. ***Jonjo & A.J. O'Neill***

Conclusion: *Smashing type on looks who won the last of his three bumpers with something in hand and looks destined for better things over hurdles for his new yard*

Mumbles (Ire) h98

6 b.g. Mahler – She's Got Grit (Ire) (Flemensfirth (USA))

2023/24 h23.9s^3 h23.9d^4 h20v^2 h19.5v* h15.8v^2 h19.2v* h20v^4 Mar 31

Mumbles has much in common with another of our *Fifty*, Mahland, beyond the fact that they're both by the same sire Mahler. Like Mahland, Mumbles is a mudlark who races prominently or makes the running and, while he's yet to really get the opportunity to prove it, he gives the impression that he too will be suited by a good test of stamina. He has quickly established himself as a Ffos Las regular, with seven of his ten starts to date having come at the Welsh track that's only 20 or so miles from the village on Swansea Bay that he's named after. Ironically, though, both his wins last season came on his only two runs elsewhere.

After three modest runs the previous season over shorter trips which earned him an initial BHA mark of 87, Mumbles had his first two starts of 2023/24 in handicaps at Ffos Las over three miles. On both occasions he gave the impression that he was suited by the longer trip but that the steadily-run nature of both those races—the first early in the season in May and the next after a summer break in October—was against him. Despite that, he was campaigned over shorter distances for the remainder of the season, albeit under testing conditions each time. Mumbles' first run of the season away from Ffos Las brought him a wide-margin victory in a handicap at Chepstow in January. Sent off favourite in a field of 12, Mumbles led on the bridle on the home turn and came well clear of just three other finishers in a strongly-run race given the conditions. Turned out under a penalty back at Ffos Las just eight days later, Mumbles ran well to finish second despite lacking the pace of the winner back at two miles, but he doubled his tally with a beating of the unenthusiastic Sangiovese in a four-runner contest at Fontwell in March when stepped back up in trip. He was only fourth back at Ffos Las on his final start of the campaign but that was another steadily-run race that wasn't in his favour.

There's stamina on both sides of Mumbles' pedigree as his dam She's Got Grit had fairly useful form over fences in Ireland at up to three miles. That being the case, there's every reason to think he'll be suited by three miles himself given the chance over fences. ***Evan Williams***

Conclusion: *Mudlark who went the right way over hurdles last term but gives the impression a combination of fences and a return to longer distances can bring out more*

Myretown (Ire) h118p

7 b.g. Dylan Thomas (Ire) – Miss Platinum (Ire) (Oscar (Ire))
2023/24 h16v^{2} h20.5v^{F} h20.9s* Mar 10

It would be asking a lot for Carron and Bruce Wymer to have another horse as talented as Ahoy Senor, the dual Grade 1 winner who has amassed more than £450,000 in prize-money, but in Myretown they have a novice chase prospect to be excited about.

Connections have had to be patient with Myretown who was off the course for 15 months after finishing fourth on his bumper debut at Hexham in October 2022, but he shaped well on his first start over hurdles at Ayr in January when a clear-cut second behind the odds-on favourite. Myretown was understandably keen on that return to action but he channelled his energy much more efficiently when upped in trip at Ayr the following month and looked unlucky not to get off the mark as he was a length in front and had yet to be asked for his effort when falling at the final flight. It didn't take long for Myretown to make amends, though, as he readily landed the odds at Kelso four weeks later. A few in behind offered some promise but Myretown was essentially in a different league to his rivals and drew clear in impressive fashion to score by 11 lengths.

Myretown, who like Ahoy Senor is a winning pointer by Dylan Thomas, showed plenty of ability during a light campaign over hurdles last season and looks likely to flourish over fences. One slight niggle is that he showed a tendency to lug left at Kelso, so it remains to be seen how he will handle going the other way, but he's certainly one to be positive about on the whole, and it's not hard to imagine this front-runner taking plenty of his rivals out of their comfort zone. ***Lucinda Russell***

Conclusion: *Winning pointer who represents the same connections as Ahoy Senor and showed ability during a light hurdling campaign; exciting prospect for novice chasing*

One Big Bang (Ire) h121p

6 gr.g. Masked Marvel – Boston du Berlais (Fr) (Turgeon (USA))

2023/24 h20v^4 h24v^3 h24v^4 h23.7s^{pu} h24.3d* h23.3v* Apr 6

One Big Bang would have been an unlikely-looking candidate as a 'Horse To Follow' for much of last season but his fortunes took a significant turn for the better following a change of stables in the spring and he looks one to keep on side now that he's found the habit of winning races. He'd shown ability for his previous handler in Ireland, Paul Tobin, especially once his stamina was really tested as he made the frame in a couple of three-mile handicap hurdles run on heavy ground, at Limerick and Fairyhouse, over the winter. But he ran poorly when tongue tied for a maiden at Punchestown on his next start and appeared to have reached the limit of his progress.

But his subsequent move to James Owen in Newmarket was clearly beneficial as One Big Bang showed plenty of improvement to win both his starts for his new stable under claiming amateur Alex Chadwick. Owen was one of our 'Rising Stars' in last year's Horses To Follow and enjoyed a very successful first jumps season as a full licence holder, training a total of 38 winners last term. They included useful juvenile hurdler Burdett Road, another useful hurdler in Too Friendly who won good handicaps in the summer at Market Rasen and Perth, and Father of Jazz who ran up an early-season hat-trick over hurdles.

Improvement was clearly expected from One Big Bang on his first start for new connections as he was gambled on for a novice handicap at Haydock at the end of March when sent off the 6/4 favourite. He duly ran away with the contest by eight lengths, travelling well and staying on strongly to draw clear from the last from unexposed runner-up Best Life. Just a week later, One Big Bang faced just two rivals, one of those a 33/1-shot, in a novice hurdle at Uttoxeter and readily followed up. Main rival Livin On Luco didn't knuckle down properly but One Big Bang still impressed with how comfortably he dealt with that fairly useful opponent and he looks a useful performer in the making, including over fences. By St Leger winner Masked Marvel, also the sire of the latest Stayers' Hurdle winner Teahupoo, One Big Bang is out of a half-sister to the Hennessy and Aintree Bowl winner Madison du Berlais. ***James Owen***

Conclusion: *Showed much-improved form to win both starts in the spring after joining a stable that's very much on the up and he could have more to offer*

One More Stroke (Ire) h115

5 b.g. Pour Moi (Ire) - Square Sphere (Ire) (Oscar (Ire))
b16s^{2} h19.3s* h17s* h16.9v^{3} Apr13

Untapped stamina reserves offer hope that there's more to come from the lightly raced One More Stroke. He was runner-up on both starts in Irish points and is out of a useful mare who won over three miles, so it was perhaps unsurprising that he saw things out thoroughly when making a successful hurdling debut over just shy of two and a half miles at Catterick in January. It was a surprise, though, to see him dropped in trip for his final two starts of the campaign and, even though he came out on top in one of those races, he remains capable of raising his level when stepping back up in trip.

One More Stroke was a promising second in a Musselburgh bumper on his debut under Rules and went one better over hurdles at Catterick where he showed a fine attitude as well as a good deal of stamina to run down the favourite after that one had made a mess of the last. The style of that success, allied with One More Stroke's profile, marked him out as one who would have no problem staying at least two and three-quarter miles, but his next assignment came in a novice hurdle over just two miles and one furlong at Carlisle. He was good enough to prevail there, though his task was helped by the favourite's departure at the second last (when One More Stroke seemed to be going slightly better) and he had to work harder than looked likely from that point, for all he always seemed to be finding enough inside the final half-furlong. He was kept to a similar trip for his handicap debut and final start of the campaign at Newcastle but on that occasion the emphasis on speed appeared to catch him out and he was relegated to last of the three finishers on the run-in, reinforcing the view that he'll benefit from stiffer tests.

It's also worth noting that the McCain stable endured a difficult campaign last term and was well down on the total number of winners from the previous two seasons, so that paints One More Stroke's promising start in an even better light. ***Donald McCain***

Conclusion: *Made a pleasing start over hurdles last season and can raise his game when presented with stiffer tests of stamina*

Party Vibes (Ire) h113p

6 b.m. Mahler – Flame of Dixie (Ire) (Beneficial)
2023/24 h16v^{2} h15.8v^{2} h15.2s* h16.6s* h20.5d^{6} h16.5s Apr 12

Party Vibes proved enthusiastic, uncomplicated and willing under pressure during her first season of racing and those traits, combined with a good jumping technique, should ensure that she continues to reward her followers and connections.

Her likeable way of going about things has been evident from the outset. On her debut over hurdles at Chepstow in November she jumped fluently and travelled with purpose at the head of affairs, and she didn't lie down when overtaken by the winner on the approach to the last. It was a similar story on her next outing at Uttoxeter, but Party Vibes gained a deserved success at Wincanton on Boxing Day and then showed improved form to follow up at Market Rasen in February, again impressing with her jumping.

That upwardly-mobile profile ensured that Party Vibes was among the market leaders for the valuable EBF National Hunt Mares' Novices' Hurdle on her handicap debut at Newbury in March, but she understandably found it more difficult to dominate in that 17-runner field and she possibly did too much too soon on her first try at two and a half miles. She ultimately weakened into sixth but may have finished in the frame had she not been badly hampered at the final flight while typically trying her best to respond.

More patient tactics were employed in a strongly run and competitive handicap hurdle back down in trip and against the geldings at Aintree's Grand National Festival. She failed to get involved, but she was again noted giving her all and that tenacious

Party Vibes puts in a typically assured leap at Aintree

attitude will continue to be a big asset. She's a lengthy sort with more presence than most mares, so she appeals as the type to take well to chasing and connections will have plenty of options. ***Henry Daly***

Conclusion: *Likeable mare whose uncomplicated running style and willing response to pressure should help her achieve further success; remains unexposed at around 2½m*

Potters Charm (Ire) b108p

5 b.g. Valirann (Fr) – Autumn In New York (Ire) (Shantou (USA))
2023/24 b15.8v* Mar 31

Some very good jumpers have begun their careers with a winning debut in a bumper at Ffos Las, among them dual Liverpool Hurdle winner Whisper, Mares' Hurdle winner Marie's Rock, Irish Grand National winner Shutthefrontdoor, Aintree regular Vieux Lion Rouge and Blaklion, whose wins for Nigel Twiston-Davies included the RSA Novices' Chase (now known as the Brown Advisory) and the Becher Chase. Blaklion spread-eagled his field on heavy ground when winning his bumper under Sam Twiston-Davies at the Welsh track at the end of March in 2014 and, ten years later virtually to the day, the same trainer and jockey were successful in a similar event with Potters Charm.

Potters Charm didn't win by quite so far as Blaklion on his debut but he still had 11 lengths to spare at the line and was most impressive. Travelling strongly towards the rear of the six-runner field, Potters Charm crept closer at halfway, disputed the lead with three furlongs to run, went on two furlongs out and then quickened clear to justify 2/1 favouritism ahead of Evan Williams' newcomer King of Thieves who was next in the betting. The first two had each been runner-up on their only start in Irish points. Potters Charm had finished second to Mulinas the previous November, the winner later joining Paul Nicholls and finishing placed in both his bumpers in the spring. Potters Charm was following in the footsteps of The Jukebox Man who'd won the same bumper the year before on his second start. He went on to finish second in the Albert Bartlett and the Sefton Novices' Hurdle last spring and Potters Charm could well be up to contesting the top staying novice hurdles himself judged on the promise he showed at Ffos Las.

Bought by Willie Twiston-Davies for £105,000 as a four-year-old after that sole run in points, Potters Charm is by Valirann whose best jumper to date is Paul Nicholls' smart hurdler Knappers Hill, also winner of last season's Rising Stars Novices' Chase. Potters Charm's dam Autumn In New York is an unraced half-sister to three winners, including fair staying hurdler Earth King, while his grandam, also unraced, was a half-sister to Willie Mullins' smart staying novice chaser Measureofmydreams who won the Ten Up Novice Chase and finished third in the National Hunt Chase. ***Nigel Twiston-Davies***

Conclusion: *Impressive winner of a Ffos Las bumper in testing conditions on his only start under Rules; he's an exciting prospect for novice hurdles*

President Scottie (Ire) h118p

6 b.g. Milan – Kinard True (Ire) (Snurge)

2023/24 h16s^3 h20.5v^2 h20.5v* h24.3s* h24.3d^4 Apr 20

Former champion conditional Danny McMenamin enjoyed his best season yet in 2023/24 with a total of 49 wins, with the highlight coming aboard Tommy's Oscar who carried 12-0 to victory in the valuable Scotty Brand Handicap Chase on Scottish Grand National day which was McMenamin's ninth success on Ann Hamilton's very smart chaser. Later on the same card, McMenamin finished fourth in a hotly-contested novice handicap hurdle on the Nicky Richards-trained President Scottie who supplied his jockey with two wins earlier in the season and should provide him with more winning opportunities this term.

Apart from on his bumper debut, President Scottie has been ridden by McMenamin on all his starts and the partnership has yet to finish out of the frame. Third on his last couple of starts in bumpers the previous season, President Scottie progressed over hurdles last term in line with increasing tests of stamina. He made an encouraging hurdles debut at Ayr when third over an inadequate two miles, went one place better there over another half-mile next time and then improved again to get off the mark over the same course and distance in February. President Scottie needed luck on his side, though, as he was beginning to look held in second when leader Myretown (an impressive winner next time and also part of our *Fifty*) fell at the last, leaving President Scottie a long way clear. On his only start of the season away from Ayr, President Scottie then followed up on his handicap debut at Haydock in March when stepped up to three miles for the first time. Looking to have been let in lightly by the handicapper and sent off the 2/1 favourite, President Scottie won what proved a rather farcical contest as all the flights in the home straight were omitted because of the low sun but he led approaching the final furlong and was driven out to beat North Parade by three and a quarter lengths.

Back at Ayr on Scottish Grand National day, President Scottie ran right up to his best in a race won by Willie Mullins' raider Chosen Witness. A lengthy, chasing type, he remains one to follow and will make particular appeal over fences this term. His dam Kinard True, a winning pointer, is the dam of two other winners, including Rob The Getaway, a fairly useful chaser at around two and a half miles. ***Nicky Richards***

Conclusion: *Reliable type who progressed with distance over hurdles and looks the sort to do at least as well over fences*

Punta Del Este (Fr) h132

5 ch.g. Gentlewave (Ire) – Cap d'Ombree (Fr) (Kapgarde (Fr))

2023/24 h16v^{2} h16v^{3} h18.9v* h24.3v^{pu} h23.3v h21.4s* Apr 19

Most of Dan Skelton's winners in a season when he was pushing hard for the trainers' championship were, of course, ridden by brother Harry. But the second-busiest jockey for the Skelton team last season was conditional Tristan Durrell, the champion amateur in 2021/22, who contributed 11 winners to his stable's total. The highlight of Durrell's season came at Kempton in January when he not only won the richest race of his career, the Lanzarote Handicap Hurdle on 33/1-shot Jay Jay Reilly, but completed his first double, having already won on Flegmatik, on a day when the stable had six winners in total around the country.

Another of Durrell's winners last season came aboard useful handicap hurdler Punta del Este whom he rode in all his races bar his final start. He probably didn't ride an easier winner all season, in fact, as Punta del Este left some largely below-form rivals trailing in his wake as he came home 21 lengths clear in heavy ground at Haydock at the end of December. Strong in the betting that day, Punta del Este looked suited by a first try beyond two miles. He'd been placed on both his previous starts last season, finishing second of four at Wetherby and then third in a better race at Sandown when not running to the same level.

Punta del Este was inevitably hit hard by the handicapper for his wide-margin win at Haydock and he struggled on his next two starts when stepped up further in trip, in a Pertemps qualifier back at Haydock and a valuable contest at Uttoxeter. But Punte del Este bounced back to form dropped back in distance on his final start at Ayr in April when springing a 25/1 surprise, this time with Kielan Woods in the saddle. Harry Skelton rode the stable's better-fancied Theformismighty but he was only fourth as outsiders fought out the finish with Punte del Este getting to long-time leader The Four Sixes to win by a length and a half. That was a useful effort from Punta del Este and makes him a contender for good handicaps at around two and a half miles this season. He has done most of his racing on soft and heavy ground and was tongue tied for his last couple of starts, as he was when successful in France earlier in his career. ***Dan Skelton***

Conclusion: *Flopped on both starts at around 3m last season but won twice over shorter and may have more to offer in handicap hurdles*

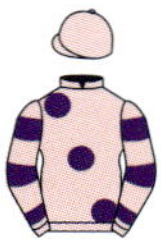

Regent's Stroll (Ire) b108

5 b.g. Walk In The Park (Ire) – Pretty Puttens (Ire) (Snurge)

2023/24 b15.7g* b16.3d* Mar 23

At £175,000, Regent's Stroll wasn't exactly a cheap purchase when joining Paul Nicholls' stable as an unraced three-year-old. But having won both his bumpers in the colours of Chris Giles in the manner of one destined for better things over jumps, it took considerably more to retain him at Ditcheat when he went through the sale ring at Doncaster for a second time in July. He was one of 11 lots sold by Giles in a dispersal of his string, eight of which were bought back by Nicholls and agent Tom Malone for other owners in the yard. Much the most expensive of those was Regent's Stroll whose £660,000 price tag broke the record for the most expensive jumper in training. At current exchange rates, that's around £30,000 more than the €740,000 which had taken Grade 1-winning novice hurdler Caldwell Potter from Gordon Elliott to Ditcheat earlier in the year. Like Caldwell Potter, Regent's Stroll will continue his career for owners involving John Hales, Jed Mason and Sir Alex Ferguson.

Regent's Stroll made a winning debut at Ascot in November and, though it took him a while to get the better of Nicky Henderson's newcomer Tradecraft by two and a half lengths, he did well in the circumstances as the steadily-run six-runner contest

Regent's Stroll is driven out to make a winning debut at Ascot

was probably more of a test of speed than ideal. It was another four months before Regent's Stroll was seen out again in the valuable Goffs UK Spring Sale Bumper at Newbury. He was one of only seven in the field of 20 with previous experience and had been the most expensive purchase in a race confined to graduates of that sale. He was also the only five-year-old in the line-up and shared favouritism with the well-backed Wincanton winner Crest of Fortune trained by Anthony Honeyball. The tall Regent's Stroll stood out beforehand, though, and built on his debut promise. Initially unable to quicken in the straight, he stayed on again to regain his earlier lead a furlong out and drew clear to beat Alan King's newcomer Don't Mind If I Do by five lengths.

Newbury, of course, was also the scene of two of Denman's mightiest performances to win the Hennessy Gold Cup. Regent's Stroll is out of a half-sister to Nicholls' 2008 Cheltenham Gold Cup winner so his long-term future lies over fences, but he can make an impact in novice hurdles first. ***Paul Nicholls***

Conclusion: *Out of a half-sister to Denman and won both his bumpers before changing hands for a record sum to remain with Paul Nicholls; he's an exciting prospect*

Sans Bruit (Fr) c139p

6 b.g. Triple Threat (Fr) – Swedish Dancer (Ire) (Teofilo (Ire))
2023/24 h25.4s c21.9s h19.4g h16s c16s^2 c15.8s* c16.5d^3 Apr 20

Sans Bruit may translate as 'without noise' but we are very much expecting this bold-jumping front-runner to make his presence felt in a two-mile handicap chase division that is perennially the weakest.

Sans Bruit, a useful sort over hurdles and fences in France for David Cottin, disappointed in a couple of handicap hurdles on his first two starts for Paul Nicholls. However, he shaped much better in a handicap chase at Chepstow where he was only denied by three-quarters of a length after impressing with how enthusiastically he travelled. Sans Bruit had raced on the heels of the leaders at Chepstow but, ten days later at Aintree, was allowed to stride on in the Red Rum Handicap Chase and produced a powerful display to score by four lengths. Propelled by a series of slick jumps, Sans Bruit was able to gallop his rivals into submission and he found plenty under Bryony Frost to see off a dangerous-looking challenge from Saint Roi, who was then only narrowly denied in a similar event at the Punchestown Festival.

Frost attempted to replicate the tactics that had served Sans Bruit so well at Aintree when the pair were reunited at Ayr only nine days later, but her mount failed to jump with the same fluency and ultimately weakened into third. Sans Bruit was hassled for the lead at Ayr, which may have contributed to the more untidy round, but it's also possible that his big effort at Aintree had slightly taken the edge off him. Either way,

Sans Bruit put in a superb round of jumping in the Red Rum Handicap Chase

he's better judged on his performance in the Red Rum. Sans Bruit was placed in a Grade 2 over two and three-quarter miles for David Cottin in France but has looked much more about speed than stamina since joining Nicholls and he has all the tools to suggest he'll win more valuable handicaps at around the minimum trip. ***Paul Nicholls***

Conclusion: *Impressive winner of the Red Rum Handicap Chase who could still have more to offer for his leading yard; capable of landing another valuable handicap in a weak division*

Ski Lodge (Ire) b101

5 b.g. Gatewood – Ballygill Countess (Ire) (Presenting)

2023/24 b16v^2 b16v* Jan 30

Noel Fehily retired from riding in 2019 after a career which included winning a couple of King George VI Chases on Silviniaco Conti and Champion Hurdles on Rock On Ruby and Buveur d'Air. The former jockey now runs the Noel Fehily Racing Syndicates in partnership with friend and former weighing-room colleague David Crosse and has enjoyed success on the big stage in that capacity, too, with Tahmuras winning the Tolworth Novices' Hurdle at Sandown and Love Envoi counting the Dawn Run Mares' Novices' Hurdle at the Cheltenham Festival among her seven wins over jumps.

Among the younger horses who ran in the syndicate's colours last season, Ski Lodge looks one of the most promising judged on a couple of runs in bumpers at Chepstow during the winter for Alan King. He made an encouraging start when runner-up on his debut in December, though the way things unfolded he had little chance with the David Pipe-trained newcomer Jurancon who readily pulled clear to win by eight lengths. From further back in the field, Ski Lodge made steady headway before getting outpaced but stayed on again in the final furlong to snatch second late on. Jurancon won again under a penalty at Hereford later in the season while Ski Lodge himself went one better back at Chepstow the following month when conditions were again very testing. While Ski Lodge had shown most of those with bumper form, the 7/4 favourite was Bobby's Nelson for Philip Hobbs and Johnson White who, like Ski Lodge, had been runner-up on his only start in Irish points. Ski Lodge went on in the back straight but was joined by the favourite after the home turn before the pair went hammer-and-tongs for the full extent of the straight. It was only in the last 25 yards or so that Ski Lodge gained an advantage, having half a length to spare at the line with the remainder finishing well strung out.

Ski Lodge is the only British-trained runner so far for his sire Gatewood, a smart middle-distance performer by Galileo whose wins for John Gosden included the Wolferton Handicap at Royal Ascot, while his dam Ballygill Countess, although just poor herself, was a sister to the 2015 Pertemps Final winner Call The Cops. He's one to look forward to over hurdles. ***Alan King***

Conclusion: *Showed plenty of resolution to win the second of two starts in bumpers in testing conditions at Chepstow; goes novice hurdling with an encouraging profile*

Tellherthename (Ire) h132

5 b.g. Malinas (Ger) – Whos To Know (Ire) (Bravefoot)

2023/24 h15.7d^{2} h15.8g* h16.5v^{pu} h15.8s* h16.4v Mar 12

As detailed in the entry on the same owners' Monty Bodkin, Tellherthename is another who has made the short move over the summer from Ben Pauling to fellow Cotswold trainers Jonjo and AJ O'Neill. Both horses made their debut for their former yard on the same card at Ascot in November and ran with promise to finish second, Monty Bodkin in a bumper and Tellherthename in a novice hurdle. It turned out that Tellherthename bumped into the best British-trained novice of the season, Jango Baie, and very nearly beat him, leading at the last but headed on the line to be beaten a nose after the pair had pulled clear. They met again in the new Formby Novices' Hurdle at Aintree on Boxing Day, by which time Tellherthename had easily landed the odds in a maiden at Huntingdon. But while Jango Baie followed up his Ascot success, Tellherthename, who actually started the shorter price of the pair, dropped away quickly from the home turn and was pulled up having lost his action.

He wasn't the only disappointment on the Aintree card for his stable as Monty Bodkin underperformed there too, but the yard was in much better form again when Tellherthename had his sights lowered back at Huntingdon less than three weeks later. As on his previous visit, he landed very short odds, making all the running and still full of running at the line where he had 14 lengths to spare over Dartmoor Pirate who was soon to show fairly useful form himself. After missing the Betfair Hurdle because of testing ground, Tellherthename made his second attempt at Grade 1 company in the Supreme Novices' Hurdle but this time seemed beaten on merit as one of only three British-trained novices in the field, making much of the running as usual before weakening to finish last of the ten who completed.

Raced only at two miles over hurdles, Tellherthename has plenty of pace, so much so that his owners were apparently seriously considering trying him on the Flat with Ed Dunlop over the summer, but that would have been an unorthodox plan for one who was bought for £200,000 after winning his only start in Irish points and is a lengthy chasing type on looks. Held in high regard by his former trainer, he's an exciting prospect for novice chases. ***Jonjo & A.J. O'Neill***

Conclusion: ***Didn't do himself justice in Grade 1 company but ran Jango Baie very close first time up and it would be no surprise if he makes more of an impact at a higher level in novice chases***

The Famous Five (Fr) h119+

6 b.g. Camelot – Palme Royale (Ire) (Red Ransom (USA))
2023/24 h21.2s^3 h15.8s^3 h21.2s^4 h15.5v* h16.7v* Mar 23

Like many horses trained by Venetia Williams, The Famous Five was bred and raced in France but he's far from being a typical import for his stable. By 2000 Guineas and Derby winner Camelot, he's bred for the Flat, not jumps, and was campaigned successfully on the level by Henri-Alex Pantall, winning twice over middle-distances as a three-year-old, showing fairly useful form, and finishing third in a listed race at Longchamp. He might not have ordinarily been on his trainer's radar, therefore, but The Famous Five raced in France in the colours of bloodstock agent Guy Petit who has a long-standing connection with the Williams yard, having sourced, among others, its Grand National winner Mon Mome and current stable star L'Homme Presse. The Famous Five changed hands at an online sale for €250,000 in the summer of his three-year-old season and the following February made his hurdles debut in the Adonis Juvenile at Kempton.

It was a stiff introduction to hurdling for The Famous Five, especially as he looked to have a lot to learn about jumping, but, following that inauspicious debut for current connections, he showed much more ability when returning from the best part of two years off last autumn. His first three starts all came at Ludlow, including a couple of tries over two miles and five furlongs. But he gave the impression the trip was stretching him and he duly got off the mark when dropped back to around two miles after the turn of the year. All the rage in the betting, The Famous Five was sent off at even-money against five rivals in a handicap at Leicester in January and impressed with how he went about things in deteriorating conditions. Travelling strongly, The Famous Five loomed up in the straight before he was produced to lead at the last and he went on to win readily by two and a quarter lengths from one of the pace-setters.

Two months later, The Famous Five followed up at the same odds in another handicap, this time at Bangor, again on heavy ground. Up with the pace throughout, he won in similar style, quickening clear again on the run-in from the thriving El Jefe who won his fifth race of the season two starts later at Aintree's Grand National meeting. A strong, compact gelding, The Famous Five is capable of winning more races in the mud at around two miles. ***Venetia Williams***

Conclusion: ***Flat-bred gelding who returned from a lengthy absence last term, proving best at 2m and readily winning a couple of handicap hurdles in the mud; there's the potential for more to come***

Titan Discovery h123

6 b. or br.g. Pether's Moon (Ire) – It's A Discovery (Ire) (Grand Plaisir (Ire))
2023/24 h17.1s^4 h16.5d^2 h15.7g* h19.8d^2 h19.8s* h21d^2 h20.3g^6 Apr 17

Robbie Llewellyn, who features in our Rising Stars section, enjoyed a breakthrough season in 2023/24 when sending out 25 winners from 107 runners at a highly creditable strike rate of 23%. One horse who was a fine advertisement for the trainer's talent was Titan Discovery whose gradual progress resulted in two wins and offers hope of another significant contribution this term.

After showing ability to finish runner-up in two bumpers in the early months of 2023, Titan Discovery was too fresh on his return from a seven-month break on his hurdling debut at Carlisle in October, but he stepped forward on that when runner-up in another novice at Taunton and then showed a big chunk of improvement to make a successful transition to handicaps at Ascot, despite running green and not looking like the finished article.

On his next outing at Sandown, Titan Discovery was no match for the very progressive Jingko Blue who proved miles ahead of the handicapper, but he showed further improvement to fare best of the rest and stayed the longer trip well on his first attempt at two and a half miles. Back over the same course and distance a couple of weeks later, and without anything of Jingko Blue's calibre to worry about, Titan Discovery took advantage of a drop in class to justify strong support and run out an emphatic winner. He faced a much tougher assignment on his penultimate start of the campaign in a

Titan Discovery scoots away from his rivals up the Sandown Hill

well-contested handicap hurdle at Kempton in March but emerged with plenty of credit in second behind a rival from the red-hot Dan Skelton yard that secured first run, and he performed to a similar level when a close-up sixth in another competitive affair at Cheltenham on his final start of the season.

Titan Discovery has shown that he can make his presence felt in good-quality handicap hurdles, but his attitude and physique suggest that he should fare at least as well over fences, so his astute trainer will have plenty of options. ***Robbie Llewellyn***

Conclusion: *Progressed well over hurdles during a successful campaign and will remain competitive; switch to chasing could unlock further opportunities*

Traprain Law (Fr) c140p

6 gr.g. Martaline – Pina (Fr) (Kapgarde (Fr))

2023/24 c16.5g^3 c17.1v* c16.4g^5 c16.5v* c16.5d^2 Apr 20

Dual Grand National-winning trainer Lucinda Russell is understandably most closely associated with staying chasers but in Traprain Law she has a speedier sort to be positive about. Traprain Law, described by Timeform as a neat gelding, may not be an obvious chaser on looks like many of the tall, lengthy sorts that Russell tends to have in her yard, but he enjoyed an excellent first campaign over fences last season and is expected to continue on his upward curve for a while longer.

French recruit Traprain Law had shown progressive form over hurdles during his first campaign for Russell in the 2022/23 season, winning three times on ground ranging from good to firm to heavy according to Timeform's judgement of the going. He carried on the good work last season and quickly proved himself a better chaser than hurdler when posting a dominant six-length success in a Kelso handicap on just his second start over fences, looking value for at least double that margin after coasting up the run-in. That was a weak affair contested by largely exposed sorts and Traprain Law understandably found things more difficult when pitched into a much higher-calibre handicap from his 10 lb higher mark at Doncaster, but he found that experience aiding his development and he soon bounced back with an emphatic win in novice handicap company at Ayr. As had been the case at Kelso, Traprain Law really impressed with how fluently he travelled, going through the race like one well worth another crack at a valuable prize. He was given that shot in the premier handicap on Ayr's Scottish Grand National card and he produced his best effort yet even though he was picked off by a more patiently ridden rival after he had engaged the favourite, Sans Bruit (also in our *Fifty*), from a long way out. The way he went through that suggests he's still ahead of the handicapper and he has a much more positive profile than most of the rivals he's likely to meet in two-mile handicap chases in the North. ***Lucinda Russell***

Conclusion: ***Strong-travelling two-miler whose best days are still ahead of him; versatile regards ground conditions***

Tripoli Flyer (Ire) b112

5 b.g. Getaway (Ger) – Collen Beag (Ire) (Mountain High (Ire))

2023/24 b16s^5 b16g* b17d^2 Apr 13

A year after sending out Dysart Enos to win the Nickel Coin Mares' Bumper at Aintree, Fergal O'Brien saddled the first two in the other Grade 2 bumper at the meeting when Horaces Pearl got the better of stablemate Tripoli Flyer in the Weatherbys-sponsored contest that closes Grand National day. The Connor Brace-ridden winner was the longer priced of the pair but stayed on take the lead from Tripoli Flyer in the final 50 yards after the runner-up had cruised to the front under Paddy Brennan three furlongs out but hung left in the closing stages. On Brennan's 43rd birthday, Tripoli Flyer was one of the last rides in the long and successful career of his jockey who announced his retirement four days later after winning at Cheltenham on the stable's Manothepeople.

Horaces Pearl is unbeaten in three bumpers and should do well over hurdles himself, but the year-younger Tripoli Flyer is a strong gelding and has more about him

Tripoli Flyer (blue jacket, yellow sleeves) travelled best when runner-up at Aintree

physically, so he looks at least as good a prospect for novice hurdles. Tripoli Flyer might have missed out on a good prize at Aintree but he'd already won nearly as big a pot when successful in the bumper on Lingfield's polytrack at their Winter Million fixture in January. Nicky Henderson's newcomer Kingston Pride was sent off the odds-on favourite but Tripoli Flyer found a better turn of foot after the pair had pulled clear in the straight, Tripoli Flyer again showing a tendency to hang left but going on to win by a length and a half with a gap of ten lengths to the third. That was a much-improved effort from Tripoli Flyer who had shown plenty to work on when a never-nearer fifth on his debut at Chepstow at the end of October.

Bought for €85,000 as a three-year-old at the Tattersalls Ireland Derby Sale, Tripoli Flyer is a brother to Anyharminasking, a useful handicap hurdler at up to two and a half miles for Jonjo O'Neill who has the distinction of once beating Constitution Hill in an Irish point. Their dam Collen Beag was a fairly useful hurdler in Ireland and a half-sister to Noah And The Ark who has been one of the leading jumpers in the USA in recent years, winning the Grand National Hurdle there last autumn a year after chasing home Hewick in the same contest. ***Fergal O'Brien***

Conclusion: *Denied late on by a stablemate in the Grade 2 bumper at Aintree but shaped the better of the pair and has more substance; expected to do well in novice hurdles*

Welcom To Cartries (Fr) h127

6 b.g. No Risk At All (Fr) – Nasou (Fr) (Kaldounevees (Fr))
2023/24 h19.3g^2 h21.6g* h24.4g^2 h24.3d Apr 20

Bravemansgame and Topofthegame, two of Paul Nicholls' best chasers in recent seasons, had won a point for Donnchadh Doyle so hopes were understandably high for Welcom To Cartries when he arrived at Ditcheat following a 16-length win at Borris House for the same handler. In truth, Welcom To Cartries' hurdling campaign was more solid than spectacular but it has laid the foundations for what we expect will be a successful chasing career.

Welcom To Cartries was unable to reward favouritism on his hurdling debut at Ascot in November but he shaped with plenty of encouragement and lost out by only a head to a rival whose experience probably proved decisive. Connections didn't have to wait long for compensation, however, as Welcom To Cartries won at the same venue a month later. The outcome to that maiden, contested over just shy of two and three-quarter miles, had looked in the balance halfway up the run-in but Welcom To Cartries proved strong in the finish and ultimately scored by six and a half lengths.

That performance earned Welcom To Cartries a step up in class and trip in the River Don, a Grade 2 novice which had been contested by the yard's subsequent Albert Bartlett Novices' Hurdle winner Stay Away Fay the previous season. However, just like Stay Away Fay, Welcom To Cartries had to settle for second at Doncaster. In a race run at a steady gallop on good ground that failed to test stamina as much as anticipated, Welcom To Cartries had no answer when the strong-travelling winner quickened on the approach to the second last, but he stuck to his task well to prove best of the rest.

He was well below form on his handicap debut and final start of the season at Ayr but such a display does not diminish his prospects for chasing. He's a well-made chasing type on looks and we have yet to see the best of him. ***Paul Nicholls***

Conclusion: *Winning pointer who showed useful form over hurdles but has the physique and background to do better in novice chases*

SPORTING LIFE
GET AHEAD
YOUR ULTIMATE BETTING COMPANION
Catch expert tips and previews alongside Timeform analysis, plus exclusive insight from some of racing's biggest names
DOWNLOAD THE APP FOR FREE
SL
SPORTING LIFE
Full Results
Nrs
Features
News
MATT BROCKLEBANK'S
VALUE BET
Energy looks Elliott's National jewel
Racing
4 hrs ago
ALL WEATHER ANGLE
Back Eleanor to power home
Racing
4 hrs ago
WATCH & LEARN
Did Cobden steal the Betfair Ascot Chase?
Racing
1 day ago

SECTION 2

Bioluminescence (Ire) h127+

6 b.m. Walk In The Park (Ire) – Molly Round (Ire) (Old Vic)
2023/24 h16v^2 h20v* h22.3v* h20v^{pu} Mar 31

Owner JP McManus has won three of the four editions of the Mrs Paddy Power Mares' Chase staged at the Cheltenham Festival and enjoyed a one-two in the latest renewal as Limerick Lace, trained by Gavin Cromwell, led home Dinoblue. It would be little surprise were Cromwell and McManus to have another leading contender in 2025 as Bioluminescence, who like Limerick Lace is by leading national hunt sire Walk In The Park, appeals as a mare who could thrive over fences.

Bioluminescence, a winner on her sole start in points, had only one outing in bumpers during the 2022/23 season but showed plenty of ability to finish runner-up at Limerick behind Junta Marvel who went on to land the Grade 3 mares' bumper at the Punchestown Festival. Bioluminescence also had to settle for second behind a promising rival on her hurdling debut at Navan on her reappearance last November, but she again shaped with encouragement and pulled clear of the third. She duly built on that promise to readily land a mares' maiden hurdle at Punchestown in January and then further enhanced her positive profile by following up in Grade 3 company at Limerick on the weekend before the Cheltenham Festival.

That two-and-three-quarter-mile event on heavy ground wasn't the stamina test it threatened to be as they went a steady gallop before sprinting from the second last, but Bioluminescence, who was always jumping and travelling well in a handy position, still impressed as she drew three and a quarter lengths clear. That decisive victory earned Bioluminescence another steep rise in class and she was sent off the 13/2 fourth choice in the market for the Grade 1 Honeysuckle Mares Novice Hurdle at Fairyhouse's Easter Festival, but she ran too badly to be true and was pulled up. That effort is best ignored and this sizeable mare remains a good prospect for chasing. ***Gavin Patrick Cromwell***

Conclusion: *Lightly-raced sort who fared well over hurdles but has the physique of one that should take well to chasing; looks a possible candidate for the Mares' Chase*

Brighterdaysahead (Fr) h143p

5 b.m. Kapgarde (Fr) – Matnie (Fr) (Laveron)
2023/24 h15.9s* h16.9s* h21v* h16.8s^2 h20d* Apr 13

Her name says it all. Gordon Elliott and owners Gigginstown House Stud enjoyed plenty of Grade 1 success in the past with Apple's Jade and connections may well have another high-class mare on their hands in Brighterdaysahead. She's the third Grade 1 winner that Elliott has trained out of the excellent broodmare Matnie, though Mighty Potter sadly met with a fatal fall in the spring of 2023 and Caldwell Potter was sold for a record €740,000 and sent to Paul Nicholls during the latest campaign.

But at least Elliott can look forward to further success with Brighterdaysahead who, at €310,000 as an unraced three-year-old, was no cheap buy herself. Already the winner of both her bumpers, including a valuable event at Fairyhouse, she was only beaten once in five starts in her first campaign over hurdles last season. After wins at Thurles and Down Royal in the autumn, the latter a Grade 3 contest, Brighterdaysahead completed her Cheltenham preparation by conceding 7 lb all round in the listed Apple's Jade Mares Novice Hurdle at Navan in February which she won impressively by a dozen lengths. As a result, Brighterdaysahead started a shade of odds on for the Dawn Run at the Festival, run as the Ryanair Mares' Novices' Hurdle. But there was no joy for race sponsor Michael O'Leary as Brighterdaysahead seemed to find the slow pace over the shorter trip all against her, failing to settle and then lacking the finishing speed of Golden Ace to whom she was conceding 5 lb.

But back over a longer trip in the Mersey Novices' Hurdle at Aintree, Brighterdaysahead had little trouble regaining the winning thread in the absence of her half-brother Caldwell Potter who was ruled out on the eve of the race. She didn't need to improve to beat her connections' other contender Staffordshire Knot by seven and a half lengths, but she did so in taking style. A good-topped mare, Brighterdaysahead is a chaser on looks as well as pedigree, and connections have confirmed she'll be going over fences this season—'there's no point in hanging around over hurdles with a mare like her'. ***Gordon Elliott***

Conclusion: *Very much living up to her family's high standards and had valid excuses for her only defeat to date at Cheltenham; looks likely to reach a high level over fences*

Built By Ballymore (Ire) h138

6 b.g. Flemensfirth (USA) – Morning Supreme (Ire) (Supreme Leader)
2023/24 h16s h21v* h20v* h21v h23.8v^{pu} Mar 30

Fastorslow, owned by Sean and Bernardine Mulyran and trained by Martin Brassil, lowered the colours of dual Cheltenham Gold Cup winner Galopin des Champs in the Punchestown Gold Cup for the second year running in May. With Built By Ballymore, the same connections have another horse with the potential to upset representatives from bigger yards in novice chases this season. Fastorslow and Built By Ballymore, along with a third stablemate Ose Partir, formed a small but select raiding party for connections at the latest Cheltenham Festival but it proved a luckless venture as Ose Partir was brought down in the Boodles Juvenile Handicap Hurdle, Fastorslow unseated in the Gold Cup and a gamble which saw Built By Ballymore being backed down to start 4/1 favourite for the Coral Cup went astray.

Wearing cheekpieces for his handicap debut in the Coral Cup, Built By Ballymore was possibly a bit keener than ideal but for whatever reason didn't pick up as expected when asked for his effort and finished down the field. That was in contrast to Built By

Ballymore's two starts before Cheltenham, both of which he'd won under similarly testing conditions. Clearly all the better for his reappearance at Naas the previous month and backed accordingly, Built By Ballymore got off the mark when stepped up to the Coral Cup trip in a maiden at Limerick just after Christmas. Built By Ballymore could be called the winner a good way from home in a well-run race and won easing down by a dozen lengths. A month later at Punchestown, he followed up by the same margin in a novice, though that required a much-improved effort as he showed useful form. Still with only one behind him entering the straight, Built By Ballymore's stamina kicked in late as he led approaching the last and then forged clear to win from the fairly useful Silver King.

Built By Ballymore may yet prove suited by further still but ran no sort of race when tried over three miles in a novices' handicap at Fairyhouse 17 days after Cheltenham. A strong gelding, he's a chasing type on looks and has a smart half-brother over fences in Dancing On My Own who won the Red Rum Handicap Chase at Aintree for the Mulryans in 2023 as well as another valuable two-mile handicap at Cheltenham last autumn. ***Martin Brassil***

Conclusion: ***Disappointing when sent off favourite for the Coral Cup but made a good impression in testing ground in Ireland beforehand and looks the type to do better still over fences***

Fact To File (Fr) c166p

7 b.g. Poliglote – Mitemps (Fr) (Trempolino (USA))

2023/24 c20v^2 c21.3v* c21.5s* c24.5v* Mar 13

For all his success as an owner of jumpers, JP McManus has only seen his colours carried to victory once in a Cheltenham Gold Cup and that was more than a decade ago by Synchronised in 2012. But he looks to have as strong a team of staying chasers as he's ever had to represent him this season and if there's another Gold Cup winner among them then it's most probably the very promising seven-year-old Fact To File. The bookmakers certainly think so as he's challenging stablemate Galopin des Champs, winner of the last two Gold Cups, for favouritism next March.

Fact To File had been one of the leading bumper horses in 2022/23, finishing second in the Champion Bumper, but instead of a conventional season in novice hurdles, Willie Mullins fast-tracked the strong, compact Fact To File straight to fences last season. Mullins had adopted the same approach with his first top-class chaser Florida Pearl, winner of the Royal & SunAlliance Chase in 1998 just a year after winning the Champion Bumper. Like Florida Pearl, Fact To File ended his novice chase campaign with victory in what is nowadays the Brown Advisory Novices' Chase at the Festival. It was his first try at around three miles and, once warming to his task, he put in a very fluent display, jumping the last superbly before drawing clear to beat Monty's Star by the best part of four lengths, looking every inch a chaser with Gold Cup potential.

Fact To File (right) measures one well on his way to an impressive win in the Brown Advisory Novices' Chase

Fact To File's only defeat in four starts over fences came on his chasing debut at Navan behind the smart American Mike but he shaped well and next time was a facile winner at Leopardstown just after Christmas in the same beginners' chase Galopin des Champs had won two years earlier. Like Galopin des Champs, Fact To File then followed up over the same course and distance in the Grade 1 novice registered as the Scalp at the Dublin Racing Festival, a race also won by Florida Pearl. That proved a non-event with stablemate and sole rival Gaelic Warrior out of sorts and ultimately failing to complete but that didn't detract from Fact To File's own performance as he went on to prove at Cheltenham. Sure to improve further in his second season over fences, Fact To File's Gold Cup claims should be all the stronger by next spring. ***Willie Mullins***

Conclusion: *Skipped novice hurdles and quickly proved himself a top-class chasing prospect, notably winning the Brown Advisory in the manner of one who could threaten Galopin des Champs' bid for a third Gold Cup*

Firefox (Ire) h151

6 b.g. Walk In The Park (Ire) – Cuteasafox (Ire) (Vinnie Roe (Ire))
2023/24 b16.9s* h16s* h20s^4 h16.4v^3 h16.5s^2 h16.7d^2 Apr 30

Firefox's claim to fame is that he's the only horse so far to have lowered the colours of Ballyburn. When the pair of them met in a maiden hurdle at Fairyhouse in December the betting found them hard to split in a field of 24, with Ballyburn sent off at 10/11 and Firefox at even money. Ballyburn had won both his bumpers the previous season while Firefox had just won his third bumper in a row when making a successful reappearance at Down Royal the previous month. Jumping soundly in front, Firefox made all the running and made his fitness edge count in beating Ballyburn by two and a half lengths. However, while Ballyburn won all his remaining starts, including Grade 1 contests at Leopardstown, Cheltenham and Punchestown to establish himself as much the best novice hurdler of the season, Firefox didn't win another race, but he did show smart form and was placed at all three major spring festivals.

Before that, Firefox finished fourth behind outsider Readin Tommy Wrong in the Lawlor's of Naas Novice Hurdle over two and a half miles, a trip he's bred to stay. However, he performed better back at two miles in his remaining starts, beginning with the Supreme at Cheltenham where he shaped as though he would have done better still in a more truly-run race and with better luck in running. Short of room after being shaken up in the straight, he kept on to finish five lengths third behind Slade Steel. Firefox duly improved a bit more in the Top Novices' Hurdle at Aintree but that wasn't enough to turn the tables on Supreme runner-up Mystical Power, though he did rally well after he was headed and was beaten only half a length. There was a similar result when the pair met again in the KPMG Champion Novice Hurdle at Punchestown where Firefox turned in another smart effort but found Mystical Power a length and three-quarters too good after again getting his head in front for a time. He was four and a quarter lengths clear of Slade Steel in third.

Firefox deserved plenty of credit for his consistency last term but perhaps he'll be better rewarded for that when he goes over fences. He certainly looks the type to make a chaser, being a tall, good-topped gelding, and he seems to have all the attributes to be one of the best in the novice division. ***Gordon Elliott***

Conclusion: *Took the scalp of Ballyburn on his first start last year before producing good efforts in defeat at all three big spring festivals; can make his mark in top novice chases*

Gaelic Warrior (Ger) c169

6 b.g. Maxios – Game of Legs (Fr) (Hernando (Fr))

2023/24 c18.9s* c19.5v* c21.5sur c15.9v* c16.3d^2 May 2

After finishing second on his first two visits to the Cheltenham Festival as a hurdler, it was third time lucky for Gaelic Warrior when he put up a top-class performance and the best by a novice chaser all season to win the Arkle. Gaelic Warrior was sent off the 2/1 favourite for the Arkle despite concerns about his jumping around the left-handed track (he tends to jump right) and the drop back to two miles for the first time for more than a year. His edgy demeanour beforehand in a first-time hood was a potential worry, too, but perhaps most of all he had to shrug off a poor display on his previous start at the Dublin Racing Festival where he was already well held in a match against stablemate Fact To File when unseating at the last. However, the market confidence in him before the Arkle proved well founded as Gaelic Warrior tanked along behind the pace before leading approaching the last and quickened clear on the run-in to win by eight and a half lengths from Found A Fifty with stablemate Il Etait Temps back in third. The placed horses in the Arkle went on to frank the form by winning Grade 1s at Aintree.

That was Gaelic Warrior's third win over fences after a very promising start to his campaign which had seen him win impressively on his chasing debut at Punchestown (from subsequent Cheltenham Festival and Grade 1 winner Inothewayurthinkin) and then follow up with another sparkling performance in the Grade 1 Faugheen Novice

Gaelic Warrior storms up the Cheltenham hill to land the Arkle Challenge Trophy Novices' Chase

Chase at Limerick in December where Il Etait Temps and Inothewayurthinkin followed him home. Having beaten his stablemate twice, it was therefore a shock when Gaelic Warrior was turned over by Il Etait Temps when they met again in the Barberstown Castle Novice Chase at the Punchestown Festival but that was a tactical four-runner contest which favoured the winner. Gaelic Warrior remains sure to be a force in open company at up to two and a half miles, though he has won at up to three. ***Willie Mullins***

Conclusion: *Dispelled doubts about the shorter trip and going left-handed with the best novice chase performance of the season in the Arkle; looks sure to make his mark in top races in open company*

Hgranca de Thaix (Fr) c145p

7 b.g. Saddler Maker (Ire) – Kapica de Thaix (Fr) (Kadalko (Fr))
2023/24 c16.5s^3 c16.2v^5 c16.7s^3 c19.5v* c20.2s* May 3

Willie Mullins has dominated the two-and-a-half-mile novice handicap chase at the Punchestown Festival and was seeking a sixth win in a row in a contest he had targeted with classy operators such as Kemboy, Real Steel and Asterion Forlonge. The winning sequence came to an end in the latest edition as two of Mullins' runners were pulled up, including the 4/1 joint-favourite Mister Policeman, while his only representative to complete, Tactical Move, was beaten a long way in seventh, but there was still an extremely promising winner in Barry Connell's Hgranca de Thaix.

Perceval Legallois—who is also on our Irish list—set a good gallop on rain-softened ground and it was a test that proved too much for most of the field, with only eight of the 17 runners managing to complete. Turning for home it was clear that the race concerned only Perceval Legallois and Hgranca de Thaix and, after jumping the final fence in unison, it was the latter who proved strongest up the run-in to forge four lengths clear, showing smart form in the process.

Hgranca de Thaix had been kept to trips around two miles on his first three starts as a chaser and he clearly appreciated the step up in distance to just shy of two and a half miles when getting off the mark over fences at Limerick in March. That contest had developed into something of a dash, however, and Hgranca de Thaix relished the greater emphasis on stamina at Punchestown where his strength in the finish was impressive. He has yet to be tried at three miles but a step up in trip looks on the cards as, following his Punchestown success, Connell nominated the Munster National at Limerick or Paddy Power Handicap Chase at Leopardstown as potential targets. He has the scope to improve further granted those stiffer tests of stamina. ***Barry Connell***

Conclusion: *Progressive chaser who showed smart form when beating a well-handicapped rival at Punchestown; his strength in the finish at Punchestown suggests he could have more to offer over longer trips*

Ile Atlantique (Fr) h141

6 br.g. Coastal Path – Cote Atlantique (Fr) (Nickname (Fr))

2023/24 h16v* h20s^{2} h21v^{3} h20d^{5} h16.7d Apr 30

We'll be surprised if Ile Atlantique doesn't quickly prove himself a better chaser than he was a hurdler. That's not to say that he didn't show much over the smaller obstacles—he was twice placed in Grade 1 novices—but he's a well-made gelding and every inch a chaser on looks. That's also why he remains one to be positive about this season despite his novice hurdle campaign ending on a disappointing note. Having had one run over hurdles before joining Willie Mullins from France, his new trainer evidently thought he'd benefit from a bumper campaign before resuming over hurdles. Ile Atlantique showed a high level of form in bumpers in 2022/23, winning on his Irish debut at Leopardstown's Christmas meeting and then going down narrowly to Stellar Story at Naas and Firefox at Fairyhouse who would both reach a high level in novice hurdles themselves.

Ile Atlantique resumed his hurdling career last season at Gowran in November when making all to win by a wide margin in heavy ground. That earned him a quick promotion to Grade 1 company in the Lawlor's of Naas Novice Hurdle in January where he shaded favouritism from old rival Firefox in a field of seven. However, Mullins had three outsiders in the race and one of those, Readin Tommy Wrong, caused an upset, getting up in the dying strides to beat Ile Atlantique, who had led most of the way, by a neck. Kept to two and a half miles or thereabouts, Ile Atlantique showed similar form next time in the Gallagher Novices' Hurdle at Cheltenham, though he was very much the stable's second string this time behind Ballyburn. Held up on this occasion, Ile Atlantique finished a one-paced third to the yard's top novice hurdler in a race where Mullins' runners took the first five places. At Aintree, Ile Atlantique took a strong hold under another patient ride in the more steadily-run Mersey Novices' Hurdle, finishing a below-form fifth, and he fared worse still at Punchestown, despite reverting to front-running tactics and dropping back to two miles, when trailing home last behind stablemate Mystical Power.

But Ile Atlantique will be starting out with a clean slate over fences this season with every chance of getting his career back on track. While he stays two and a half miles, he should prove just as effective bowling along over shorter, much like Energumene who has carried the same colours of Tony Bloom with such distinction. ***Willie Mullins***

Conclusion: *His season ended on a low note but he is better judged on what he showed when placed in two Grade 1 novices; has the look of one who will take well to fences*

Inthepocket c148p

7 b.g. Blue Bresil (Fr) – Egretta Island (Ire) (Heron Island (Ire))
2023/24 c17v^2 Nov 18

Take two! Inthepocket appears for the second year running in this list as a prospective top novice chaser in the hope that he'll see a bit more action than he managed last term. He made his chasing debut in a beginners' chase at Navan last November but so too did another of the previous season's leading novice hurdlers, Facile Vega. The pair dominated the betting and they duly finished one-two, with the odds-on Facile Vega winning with plenty in hand by just under four lengths. However, neither of them made the expected impact in novice chases during the rest of the season, though in Inthepocket's case that was because he wasn't seen out again after pulling muscles behind.

To recap on Inthepocket's novice hurdle campaign in 2022/23, before which he won his only start in points, he won three of his five starts, notably the Grade 2 Navan Novice Hurdle, which was his only try at much beyond two miles, and the Top Novices' Hurdle at Aintree on his final start. Inthepocket justified favouritism at Aintree, despite his rider dropping her whip, from a couple who did well kept to hurdles last season; Strong Leader, who won the Liverpool Hurdle back at Aintree, and the Champion Hurdle third Luccia. Further back in the field was Found A Fifty who returned to Aintree a year later and rounded off an excellent first season over fences by winning the Maghull Novices' Chase. Inthepocket also finished second to Il Etait Temps at the Dublin Racing Festival but ran his best race when beaten only around six lengths in fourth in the Supreme Novices' Hurdle at Cheltenham won by Marine Nationale from Facile Vega.

A useful-looking gelding, Inthepocket gives the impression that he'll improve further when stepped back up in trip from around two miles. His younger half-brother Clovis Island won over two and a half miles at Hexham in the spring, while his elder half-brother To Be Sure has done all his winning, including over fences, at around three miles. Inthepocket went close to matching his smart hurdles form at the first attempt over fences at Navan, where he shaped well and wasn't given too hard a race. Winning a similar event should be a formality before he makes his mark in graded company. ***Henry de Bromhead***

Conclusion: *Grade 1 winner as a novice hurdler and made a promising debut over fences behind Facile Vega before missing the rest of last season; remains a leading novice chaser in the making*

Jalon d'Oudairies (Fr) b116

5 b.g. No Risk At All (Fr) – Ukalee (Fr) (Equerry (USA))
2023/24 b16s* b16s* b16.4v^3 Mar 13

Jalon d'Oudairies lost his unbeaten record when sent off favourite for the Champion Bumper at the Cheltenham Festival but he shaped with plenty of promise in third, showing a bit more improvement in the process, and he has the physique of one who should do well over jumps. Between them, Willie Mullins and Gordon Elliott had the first seven home in the Champion Bumper, with Jasmin de Vaux, who was providing Mullins with his hundredth Festival winner, chased home by Romeo Coolio who was the outsider of Elliott's three runners. But while the first two came from off the pace, Jalon d'Oudairies was ridden more prominently and led entering the straight before being headed over a furlong out.

Jalon d'Oudairies had just about the best form going into the Champion Bumper. Sent off favourite for his bumper debut at Fairyhouse in December, Jalon d'Oudairies looked a good prospect on his first start under Rules, impressing with how he quickened clear of his rivals after leading on the bridle and going on to win readily by five lengths from Major Barry. Later in the month, Jalon d'Oudairies followed up at Leopardstown where he faced a notable rival in Mullins' Redemption Day who was having his first start for 20 months and had last been seen chasing home stablemate Facile Vega in the 2022 Champion Bumper at Punchestown. Redemption Day looked the most likely winner approaching the final furlong but proved a bit too fresh after his lengthy absence and Jalon d'Oudairies saw off that threat to win by two and three-quarter lengths.

The Champion Bumper wasn't actually Jalon d'Oudairies' first visit to the Cheltenham Festival as he and Romeo Coolio had been the joint-top lots when selling for £420,000 at the Tattersalls Cheltenham Festival Sale in 2023. In Jalon d'Oudairies' case, that was just four days after he'd made a winning debut in a point which clearly impressed the Gigginstown team. Jalon d'Oudairies' immediate family is nothing to write home about, but he's by No Risk At All whose jumpers are headed by top-class chaser Allaho and include Champion Hurdle winner Epatante. More distant family members include Classic Chase winner Ladalko and Galway Plate runner-up Darasso. ***Gordon Elliott***

Conclusion: ***Expensive Gigginstown purchase who won his first two bumpers in the manner of a very good prospect and did nothing to alter that view when third at Cheltenham***

Kopek des Bordes (Fr) b110p

4 b.g. No Risk At All (Fr) – Miss Berry (Fr) (Cadoudal (Fr))
2023/24 b16v* Mar 31

The valuable Tattersalls Ireland George Mernagh Memorial Sales Bumper, run at Fairyhouse's Easter Festival and worth €60,000 to the winner, may well have thrown up a very good prospect for the second year running. Subsequent Grade 1 winner Brighterdaysahead took the prize in 2023 while the latest winner, Kopek des Bordes, also looks destined to make his mark in top novice hurdles following a hugely impressive victory that gave Willie Mullins a five-timer on the card.

Restricted to horses sold at certain Tattersalls Ireland sales, the latest renewal attracted a couple of runners from Britain. Unlike most of the field, Clap of Thunder for

Nigel Twiston-Davies and We're Red And Blue for Jonjo O'Neill had some experience already and both finished in the money, coming second and fourth respectively, but the strong pace by bumper standards in what were testing conditions meant that the field of 14 finished very strung out with even the fifth horse coming home more than 50 lengths adrift of the winner. One of three debutants in the line-up for Mullins, Kopek des Bordes was sent off the 15/8 favourite under Patrick Mullins who gave him a very confident ride. Travelling strongly held up, Kopek des Bordes improved to go second early in the straight and then led on the bridle over a furlong out before drawing clear of long-time leader Clap of Thunder to win by 13 lengths with another nine back to one of his stablemates Doctor Steinberg in third.

Bought for €130,000 as a three-year-old, Kopek des Bordes is by the same sire, No Risk At All, as his stable's dual Ryanair Chase winner Allaho. As we l as some useful winners in France, Kopek des Bordes is also a half-brother to Utopie des Bordes who proved a useful staying hurdler for Nicky Henderson after winning the Grade 1 Prix Maurice Gillois for four-year-old chasers at Auteuil earlier in her career. Another of Kopek des Bordes'

Kopek des Bordes won his bumper with ease and is an exciting prospect

half-sisters is the dam of Risk Belle (also by No Risk At All), a useful mare who won a Grade 3 hurdle at Fairyhouse for Mullins last season. ***Willie Mullins***

Conclusion: *Looked an exciting prospect for novice hurdles when spread-eagling his field in a valuable sales bumper on his only start*

Lecky Watson (Ire) h139

6 ch.g. Valirann (Fr) – Anno Whyte (Ire) (Stowaway)
2023/24 h23s* h20v^2 h20s^3 h24v^5 h23.9d^5 May 1

One win from ten starts so far might not sound too promising but we're expecting the lengthy Lecky Watson's strike rate to improve once he goes over fences as he looks the type to come into his own over the larger obstacles. In any case, he deserves to have more than one win to his name and would have already had he not been demoted from first when taking the meaning of 'bumper' a bit too literally for the stewards' liking in the closing stages of a race at Punchestown. Later that season, Lecky Watson was the longest price of his stable's ten runners in the 2023 Champion Bumper at Cheltenham but outran his 80/1 odds in finishing fourth behind A Dream To Share and would have been closer still had he not been badly hampered over a furlong out when holding every chance.

Having been winless from five starts in bumpers, Lecky Watson got off the mark at the first time of asking over hurdles last season. He had to work hard to land the odds in a maiden at Thurles over a furlong short of three miles but he would have benefited from a stronger gallop. Despite dropping back to two and a half miles for his next couple of starts, Lecky Watson showed useful form in graded company, running the future Supreme winner Slade Steel to half a length in the Grade 2 Navan Novice Hurdle and then finishing third behind stablemates Readin Tommy Wrong and Ile Atlantique in the Grade 1 Lawlor's of Naas Novice Hurdle.

Clearly a free-going type, Lecky Watson was fitted with a hood at the Cheltenham and Punchestown Festivals but the headgear did little to kerb his tendency to take a strong hold. Even so he ran right up to his best to finish fifth in those three-mile Grade 1 novices. For the second year running at the Cheltenham Festival he outperformed some of his shorter-priced stablemates, this time in the Albert Bartlett Novices' Hurdle won by Stellar Story, while in a deep renewal of the War of Attrition at Punchestown he might have finished slightly closer but for an awkward jump at the last. ***Willie Mullins***

Conclusion: *Only one win to his name so far but has run well in defeat, including at the last two Cheltenham Festivals, and appeals as the type to improve his strike rate when going over fences*

Maughreen (Ire) b103p

5 b.m. Walk In The Park (Ire) – Molly's Mate (Ire) (Goldmark (USA))
2023/24 b16.2s* Jan 15

It says plenty about the impression Maughreen created on her debut at Punchestown in January that she was as short as 5/1 for the Champion Bumper until she was ruled out following a slight setback just weeks before the race. Facing 11 other mares, most of whom had already run, Maughreen was sent off the 1/2 favourite for her debut under Patrick Mullins and gave her supporters few anxious moments. Travelling strongly and moving into a prominent position before halfway, Maughreen was produced to lead over a furlong out and soon went 11 lengths clear of second favourite Harrys Annie.

Another reason for Maughreen's very short price for her debut must have been her breeding. The spelling of her name is a nod to the fact that she's related to one of the best jumpers to have been trained at Closutton as her unraced dam Molly's Mate is a half-sister to Faugheen. He too had begun his career with an impressive debut success in a Punchestown bumper under Patrick Mullins as his rider recalled after Maughreen's success. 'I think he won by 22 lengths and I got a bollocking for winning too far. At least she only won by 11 lengths, so I'm learning!'

Faugheen went on to win his first ten starts in a streak which included Festival wins in the Baring Bingham and the 2015 Champion Hurdle. He won 17 races in all, making a successful switch to fences late in his career and going close to winning for the third time at the Festival when third in the Golden Miller on what proved his final start at the age of 12. By Walk In The Park who has sired two more Mullins stars, Douvan and Min, Maughreen is a half-sister to another bumper winner, Sweettowatch, and a full sister to Blow Your Wad who showed smart form in novice chases for Tom Lacey last season, winning the Pendil at Kempton. Maughreen will make plenty of appeal in novice hurdles as she looks to have plenty of size. ***Willie Mullins***

Conclusion: *Out of a half-sister to her stable's Champion Hurdle winner Faugheen and impressed on her bumper debut before a setback ruled her out of Cheltenham*

Mozzies Sister (Ire) b108

5 b.m. Arctic Cosmos (USA) – Merryisker (Ire) (Vertical Speed (Fr))
2023/24 b16v* b16.6d^{2} May 1

Some very expensive jumpers made headlines in the sales ring earlier this year but there are still some bargains to be had at the other end of the market. Good evidence of that came in the Grade 3 mares' bumper at the Punchestown Festival. All the top Irish yards were represented but the pair who fought out it came from the smaller stables of Anthony McCann and Declan Queally with their two representatives both being four-figure purchases.

Familiar Dreams and Mozzies Sister were prominent throughout and fought out quite a dramatic finish ending up on opposite sides of the track. Familiar Dreams hung badly left over to the stand rail, with her rider dropping her whip, while Mozzies Sister, who originally challenged on Familiar Dreams' outer, had to be switched when hampered by that manoeuvre but briefly got upsides in the final furlong before going down by half a length. A stewards' inquiry left the result unaltered. While the winner was completing a four-timer in bumpers (she was subsequently sold to join Gordon Elliott for €310,000), for Mozzies Sister it was only her second start under Rules.

Brought down at the last on her point debut, it was almost a year later when she landed the odds in a similar event at Dungarvan in January having joined her current stable by then. A couple of months later and fitted with a tongue strap, she was well backed for her bumper debut in a race at Cork for female jockeys which she took in impressive fashion. Her effort in the heavy conditions was all the more praiseworthy as she stuck to the inner throughout whereas the earlier races on the card suggested it was best to take a wider route. Nonetheless, Mozzies Sister travelled strongly, regained the lead with five furlongs to run and drew well clear in the last couple of furlongs to win by 14 lengths. A €6,000 purchase as a three-year-old, Mozzies Sister is by St Leger winner Arctic Cosmos and a half-sister to a couple of fairly useful staying hurdlers, Vee Dancer and Equinus, the latter a winner at Aintree for Nigel Twiston-Davies last season. There are some good jumpers further back in her pedigree, including the very smart staying hurdler Merry Masquerade. Mozzies Sister looks set to pay her way once sent hurdling. ***Declan Queally***

Conclusion: *Will continue to hold her own against mares from the bigger yards over hurdles after showing plenty of promise in bumpers*

Mywayofthinkin (Ire) h118P

5 b.g. Flemensfirth (USA) – Sway (Fr) (Califet (Fr))

2023/24 b16d^{2} b15.7v^{2} :: 2024/25 h16d* May 21

Sway was a useful juvenile hurdler in France when JP McManus bought her during the 2009/10 season and sent her to Jonjo O'Neill. While she ended up winning twice over fences for her new connections, at Ludlow and Exeter, she failed to cut much ice in better company, including at the Cheltenham Festival where she finished down the field in the David Nicholson Mares' Hurdle and, a year later, in the now discontinued novices' handicap chase.

But if Sway didn't quite deliver on the racecourse, she has certainly come up with the goods as a broodmare. All six of her foals have now won in the green and gold hoops, four of them doing so in 2024, and two of those were successful at the latest Cheltenham Festival. After Inothewayurthinkin had been backed as if defeat was out of the question and duly hacked up in the Fulke Walwyn Kim Muir, his year-older sister Limerick Lace led home a McManus one-two when beating favourite Dinoblue in the Mares' Chase at

Cheltenham a day later. Both winners then went to Aintree, and while Limerick Lace was unable to justify being sent off joint-favourite for the Grand National, Inothewayurthinkin followed up his Cheltenham success in the Mildmay Novices' Chase, looking a high-class staying chaser in the making.

Sway was also represented successfully this year by Ilikedwayurthinkin, twice a winner over fences at Cartmel in the summer for Ben Haslam, though, like all his other siblings, he too had begun his career with Gavin Cromwell. Sway's latest foal to hit the track is Mywayofthinkin who got his hurdling career off to a perfect start in a maiden at Punchestown in May. Gordon Elliott's Omniscient set a fairly useful standard so it reflects well on Mywayofthinkin that he was able to see off that rival with much more in hand than his winning margin of a length and a quarter implies after jumping ahead at the final flight. Mywayofthinkin had finished second in both his bumpers beforehand, at Leopardstown on Boxing Day and at Navan in March. Open to plenty of improvement over hurdles, Mywayofthinkin looks another above-average jumper out of his dam and he's bred to stay a lot further than two miles in due course, with Sway's other winners including Spades Are Trumps, winner of the Ulster National over three and a half miles. ***Gavin Patrick Cromwell***

Conclusion: *Sibling of a couple of this year's Festival winners and looks another above-average jumper in the making for his dam after a cosy win on hurdling debut at Punchestown*

Perceval Legallois (Fr) c147

7 b.g. Ballingarry (Ire) – Mrs Percival (Lahib (USA))

2023/24 c18.5v* c20s^{F} c20s^{5} c21.5s^{F} c20.2s^{2} :: 2024/25 c22.5d Jul 31

Sloppy errors counted against Perceval Legallois when he failed to meet expectations in the Galway Plate—at 7/2 he was the shortest-price favourite in the race since Shaneshill was beaten at 3/1 in 2017—but he remains a chaser to be positive about and is capable of landing a valuable prize this season. It's easy to see why Perceval Legallois was sent off a strong favourite for such a well-contested and prestigious event as he had looked like a well-treated horse on his two previous outings in hand cap chases. He was 3 lb out of the weights on his handicap chase debut at Leopardstown at the Dublin Racing Festival, but he would have proved even that mark lenient had he completed as he was still right in the mix when crashing out at the final fence, though may have had to settle for second given how strongly the unexposed winner, Heart Wood, charged up the run-in. There would have been no shame in finishing second to Heart Wood, who went on to be third in the Grade 1 Mildmay Novices' Chase at Aintree, and it was a similar story in the novice handicap chase at the Punchestown Festival where he found only the progressive Hgranca de Thaix too strong.

Perceval Legallois (left) ran a fine race behind another promising chaser in Hgranca de Thaix

Perceval Legallois couldn't shake off Hgranca de Thaix, who also features on this Irish list, but there was a lot to like about how enthusiastically he travelled and how well he jumped at the head of affairs, causing every rival, bar the eventual winner, to come under pressure well before the turn for home. He wasn't nearly so fluent under a more restrained ride when eighth in the Galway Plate, and he has a couple of falls against his name, but the round he put in at Punchestown and when successful on his chasing debut at Galway show that his jumping can be an asset. Perceval Legallois is in excellent hands with Gavin Cromwell, who won a host of valuable handicap chases last season including Haydock's Grand National Trial and the Kim Muir at the Cheltenham Festival, and he will be high on the shortlist for top-end handicaps between two and a half miles and three miles. ***Gavin Patrick Cromwell***

Conclusion: *Disappointed in the Galway Plate but is better judged on his two previous efforts in handicap chases; on a good mark and can land a big prize*

Quai de Bourbon (Fr) h144p

5 b.g. Ivanhowe (Ger) – Liberalis (Fr) (Muhtathir)

2023/24 h19s* h16.5v* h20.3v³ h20.5d* Apr 20

Quai de Bourbon was unable to emulate Sir des Champs and Don Poli who both won the Martin Pipe Conditional Jockeys' Handicap Hurdle for these connections at the Cheltenham Festival, but he ran a race full of promise and appeals as one who could also make his mark in Grade 1 novice chases.

Quai de Bourbon had been unsuccessful in two runs in France for Yannick Fouin the previous season but made the perfect start for Willie Mullins at Naas in December when pulling four and a half lengths clear in the style of a potentially smart stayer. He was then made to work harder to land the odds in a conditions hurdle at Clonmel the following month, but he understandably still looked rough around the edges and seemed unsuited by the drop in trip. Granted a stiffer test of stamina at Cheltenham, Quai de Bourbon duly raised his game, despite still looking a bit green, and ran a cracker to finish third to Better Days Ahead, shaping as though he'll have no problem going further than two and a half miles. He didn't need to run to the same sort of level to make

Quai de Bourbon was in a league of his own at Ayr

the most of a good opportunity back in novice company at Ayr on his final start of the season, but it was still impressive how readily he pulled clear while looking like there was plenty in the tank.

The hugely successful association between Mullins and Gigginstown House Stud was abruptly ended in the autumn of 2016 when the owners moved their horses elsewhere following a disagreement over training fees. But Mullins has been back on the Gigginstown roster of trainers for the last couple of seasons and Quai de Bourbon, who looks very much the type to make a chaser and has untapped potential over staying trips, could perhaps be the horse who gives the partnership a first Grade 1 winner together since Apple's Jade won the Champion Four Year Old Hurdle at the Punchestown Festival more than eight years ago. ***Willie Mullins***

Conclusion: *Chasing type who won three of his four starts and was an excellent third in the Martin Pipe, a race connections have won previously with future top-class chasers*

Waterford Whispers (Ire) h137

6 b.g. Westerner – Tara Belle (Ire) (Kayf Tara)

2023/24 h16.4v* h19.8s* h20s^{2} h20.3v^{2} h20.5s^{pu} May 4

The main aim of the Martin Pipe, when it was introduced to the Cheltenham Festival in 2009, was to provide an opportunity for conditional jockeys at the year's most important meeting. But in practice, it has also become a showcase for promising young horses, as well as their riders, with Galopin des Champs and Banbridge among the recent winners. That fine record of unearthing top prospects looks set to continue as the latest renewal of the Martin Pipe looked an exceptionally strong one, with four well-backed Irish novices pulling clear, each of them looking smart performers in the making at the very least. The top three in the betting from Ireland's biggest yards duly took the first three places, though Henry de Bromhead's Waterford Whispers, sent off favourite under Mike O'Connor, had to settle for second, a length and a half behind Gordon Elliott's winner Better Days Ahead with the Willie Mullins-trained Quai de Bourbon a close-up third.

Waterford Whispers shaped very well in defeat, though his inexperience was evident late on as, having travelled powerfully and made much of the running, he first edged left on the flat before hanging right in the final 100 yards when headed. Waterford Whispers had run only four times previously, having had a considerate introduction in a big field at Fairyhouse the previous spring. Making his return in a maiden at Galway, Waterford Whispers won a shade snugly and then showed plenty of improvement, relishing the step up to two and a half miles, when following up in a novice at Fairyhouse in December from Answer To Kayf who was to complete the frame in the Martin Pipe. On his only other run before Cheltenham, Waterford Whispers improved again despite not having the race run to suit when runner-up in a novice handicap at Leopardstown later the same month, shaping as though a stronger gallop would have suited.

Further progress from Waterford Whispers after Cheltenham was anticipated when he was sent off the 2/1 favourite for a listed handicap at the Punchestown Festival but he dropped away and was eventually pulled up, reportedly having lost a shoe. But he makes plenty of appeal as a novice chaser to follow and, from the family of dual Whitbread Gold Cup winner Topsham Bay, will stay three miles. ***Henry de Bromhead***

Conclusion: *Well backed and shaped with promise when runner-up in a strong edition of the Martin Pipe; will stay further and has scope to do better still over fences*

William Munny (Ire) b115

6 b.g. Westerner – Court My Eye (Elmaamul (USA))
2023/24 b16v* b15.7v* b16.6d^{3} May 1

Barry Connell has already had a smart bumper performer make a seamless transition to becoming a Grade 1-winning novice hurdler. That was Marine Nationale who was still unbeaten when winning the 2023 Supreme Novices'. William Munny has met with defeat, but his rating of 115 is higher than what Marine Nationale earned in bumpers and he remains a very exciting prospect for novice hurdles.

Connell was clearly in no hurry with William Munny as he'd just turned six when he made his debut at Navan in January. Willie Mullins supplied the odds-on favourite for the six-runner contest but, despite taking a strong hold, William Munny dug deep and stayed on well to deny winning pointer C'Est Ta Chance by a short head. That was a promising start but it was William Munny's follow-up success in another small field at Naas just over a month later which marked him out as a seriously good prospect. This was a contest which Gordon Elliott had won the year before with subsequent Albert Bartlett winner Stellar Story, as well as with Gerri Colombe in the recent past, and he fielded the even-money favourite Wingmen, an eight-length winner over course and distance on his debut. William Munny was only fourth pick in the betting in the field of five but he put up a stunning performance, tanking through the race and showing an excellent turn of foot in the heavy ground once Finian Maguire produced him to lead in the final furlong, quickening clear to win by five lengths from Fleur In The Park with the favourite only third.

Cheltenham was seemingly never on William Munny's agenda and he duly appeared next in the Champion Bumper at Punchestown where his rivals included the Cheltenham one-two Jasmin de Vaux and Romeo Coolio. Neither of those figured, and while William Munny couldn't take advantage, he remains a very exciting prospect as little went right for him. Meeting trouble in running on more than one occasion, he eventually stayed on for third, beaten more than ten lengths behind the season's top-rated bumper performer Redemption Day. William Munny is out of a close relative to Mister McGoldrick, a high-class chaser at up to two and a half miles who had an excellent record for Sue Smith at Wetherby and was also a shock winner at the Festival when winning the Plate at 66/1. ***Barry Connell***

Conclusion: *Had excuses when third in the Grade 1 bumper at the Punchestown Festival but won his first two starts in the manner of a very exciting prospect for novice hurdles*

Zanndabad (Ire) h117p

5 b.g. Iffraaj – Zanoubiya (Ire) (Dalakhani (Ire))
2023/24 h19.8s h15.6d^{2} h19.3g^{2} Mar 24 (Jun 18 2024F^{6})

The Chester Cup has been won by some talented dual-purpose performers down the years and Zanndabad was perhaps unlucky not to add his name to the roll of honour in the latest edition. Zanndabad, who was making his return to the Flat after finishing runner-up on two of his three starts over hurdles last season, went like the best horse at the weights at Chester but was too far back in a race run at no more than a fair gallop and his late surge could only take him into a close-up third.

Given the strength Zanndabad showed in the finish at Chester, it was perhaps a shade disappointing that he couldn't sustain his challenge better over a slightly longer trip in the Ascot Stakes at Royal Ascot, though he still ran creditably in sixth and again showed enough to suggest that he has the ability to prove much better than his Irish hurdles mark of 116 when he goes back jumping.

Zanndabad had won four times on the Flat in France, showing useful form, but he proved something of a slow learner over hurdles and was unplaced in three juvenile maidens in the 2022/23 campaign. His hurdling still lacked polish last season, though he finished runner-up in a Musselburgh handicap before filling the same position in an Ascot maiden to show that he's getting to grips with the task. He essentially appeared to be outstayed by a more stoutly-bred rival over an extended two miles and three furlongs at Ascot and, given his Flat background, it could be that a strongly run race at two miles will bring out the best in him over jumps. He starts out from a low base relative to his ability and it would be little surprise were he to progress through the ranks and make his presence felt in top-end handicaps. ***Mrs C. O'Leary***

Conclusion: *Useful Flat performer who has yet to match that form over hurdles but is going in the right direction; could be one to note for a valuable handicap*

TIMEFORM
OVER 75 YEARS OF
UNRIVALLED RACE ANALYSIS
AND FORM INSIGHT
TAKE YOUR FORM STUDY TO THE
NEXT LEVEL AT TIMEFORM.COM

SECTION 3

Patrick Mullins' Horses To Follow

Sporting Life ambassador Patrick Mullins, leading amateur rider and assistant trainer at Closutton, picks out five horses trained by Willie Mullins who could be worth following.

Karniquet h113

4 ch.g. Kapgarde (Fr) - Queenjo (Fr) (Grand Tresor (Fr))

Karniquet is a new French horse we've bought. He's a four-year-old so he's not a juvenile and is going to be a novice hurdler. He's by Kapgarde and was second at Pau and Auteuil in two runs. It's obviously early days and we haven't got to peak under the bonnet at all, but he looks like a horse that should be winning plenty of races this season.

Kopek des Bordes (Fr) b110p

4 b.g. No Risk At All (Fr) - Miss Berry (Fr) (Cadoudal (Fr))

Kopek des Bordes put in one of the best bumper performances last season when he won the Tattersalls George Mernagh Bumper at Fairyhouse. He was an expensive store and he's a half-brother to a Grade 1 winner in Utopie des Bordes. He's by No Risk At All and has a lot of size and scope. His performance was one that blew me away and I'd be expecting him to take top order in the novice hurdles this season.

Maughreen (Ire) b103p

5 b.m. Walk In The Park (Ire) - Molly's Mate (Ire) (Goldmark (USA))

I'm really looking forward to getting Maughreen back on the track. She's by Walk In The Park and from the family of Faugheen and put in a huge performance when she won at Punchestown—the third and fourth home have both won since at lower levels. She has the size and scope to go on and jump hurdles and indeed fences, and you'd be hoping she could make into a Dawn Run Mares' Novices' Hurdle horse this season.

Salvator Mundi (Fr) h139p

4 b.g. No Risk At All (Fr) - Stacicaya (Fr) (Saint des Saints (Fr))

Salvator Mundi is probably an obvious one. He was second to Sir Gino at Auteuil before we bought him, and he ran a cracker first time out for us when sixth in the Triumph Hurdle. He then demolished a much weaker field at Tipperary and he looks like he could be one for the Supreme Novices' Hurdle. He's by No Risk At All, which is a help, and we would have very high hopes for him this season.

You Proof (Fr) Unraced

4 b.g. Muhtathir - Al Doha (Hawk Wing (USA))

You Proof is a fine, big, beautiful model of a horse. He's by Muhtathir, the sire of Envoi Allen, and was second in his point-to-point for Pat Doyle which is a nursery we've had a lot of luck buying from. We tried to get him out for Punchestown but he didn't make it. That could be a blessing in disguise with his size and scope, and I'd be hoping he might make into one of our top bumper horses this year. He's definitely a horse to be looking forward to for the next several years..

Daryl Jacob's Horses To Follow

Daryl Jacob, retained jockey for owners Simon Munir and Isaac Souede, picks out five horses to look out for this season, including four based in Ireland who will be carrying the famed 'double green' silks.

Balhambar (Fr) h118+

5 b.g. Almanzor (Fr) - Moojeh (Ire) (King's Best USA))

I'm riding out for Harry Derham a lot and he's a trainer going places. Balhambar is a horse who did well for the team last spring having switched yards from Michael Bell, winning at Ludlow and Bangor. He's progressive and worth following. *Harry Derham*

Bronn (Ire) h141

7 b.g. Notnowcato - Cluain Easa (Ire) (Accordion)

He's a horse I finished third on behind The Real Whacker in the 2023 Brown Advisory and things just didn't fall right for him last season. He never had the rub of the green, but I'm convinced there's a big pot in him one day on decent ground. He's joined Tom Gibney who did such a great job with Intense Raffles last season. *Tom Gibney*

Karafon (Fr) h129

4 b.g. Karaktar (Ire) - Labartoli (Ire) (Intello (Ger))

I absolutely loved this horse when I rode him at Leopardstown over Christmas when he finished fifth behind Kala Conti, Kargese and Nurburgring and can't wait to see him back in action this term. He didn't race again as we wanted to retain his novice status for the season ahead and he's one to really look forward to. *Willie Mullins*

Readin Tommy Wrong (Ire) h141

6 b.g. Authorized (Ire) - Roque de Cyborg (Ire) (High Chaparral (Ire))

I won the Grade 1 Lawlor's of Naas Novice Hurdle on him in January and you can forget his run in the Albert Bartlett when sent off favourite as he clearly wasn't right. He goes novice chasing this term and is one of our most exciting prospects in that division. *Willie Mullins*

Yeshil (Ire) b96

4 b.g. Diamond Boy (Fr) - Bugatti des Mottes (Fr) (Nidor (Fr))

A fascinating prospect for the new season. He's joined Henry de Bromhead and it's very exciting to have 'double green' horses at his yard. This fellow ran very well when second to Sermandzarak in the Goffs Defender Bumper at Punchestown and should make up into a cracking novice hurdler. *Henry de Bromhead*

Readin Tommy Wrong is one to watch out for in novice chases

TALKING TO THE TRAINERS

We asked a number of leading National Hunt trainers to pick out a chaser, hurdler and novice to follow for the coming season. Here's what they said…

Harry Fry

Wins-Runs in Britain in 2023/24	**24-143**
Highest-rated horse in training	**Boothill** Timeform Rating c160

Chaser: Hymac (c127p): "A horse that we had been looking forward to going over fences since the day we bought him. He took a couple of runs to gain confidence over the larger obstacles last season before winning well at Cheltenham in April. That was over three and a half miles and we are hopeful there is more to come from this lightly raced eight-year-old in staying handicaps."

Hurdler: Anno Power (b100p): "A dual bumper winner last season, she has shown a decent turn of foot and we are looking forward to her starting out on her hurdling

Gidleigh Park looked a bright prospect in novice hurdles last season

career. She schools well, she'll be campaigned over two miles and will hopefully be contesting black-type races before long."

Novice: Gidleigh Park (h138): "An exciting prospect who we hope can rank highly among this season's novice chasers. He has won over two miles and two and a half miles, and we will probably look to campaign him over that sort of trip having over-raced when he was stepped up to three miles in the Albert Bartlett."

Nicky Henderson

Wins-Runs in Britain in 2023/24	**91-440**
Highest-rated horse in training	**Constitution Hill** Timeform Rating h177

Chaser: Fantastic Lady (c150): "She progressed last year and put up her best ever performance in the Oaksey Chase at Sandown on her last run of the season. She will hopefully hold her own against the top mares in this category this season."

Hurdler: Constitution Hill (h177): "I certainly hope and believe he can be back to his brilliant self for this coming season. Last year was obviously disappointing as he only ran the once. It might seem obvious, but the plan is to start, as always, in the Fighting Fifth at Newcastle."

Novice: Jango Baie (h148p): "He had a very successful first season over hurdles and looks a ready-made novice chaser."

Philip Hobbs & Johnson White

Wins-Runs in Britain in 2023/24	**34-257**
Highest-rated horse in training	**Zanza** Timeform Rating c152§

Chaser: Masters Legacy (c133): "Has had a year off but as a result could be better handicapped and is a strong horse now."

Hurdler: Limier d'Arthel (b100): "Won a three-year-old AQPS bumper in France and will be running in juvenile hurdles."

Novice: Ballee (h139): "Was progressive last season and could be an exciting novice chaser."

Paul Nicholls

Wins-Runs in Britain in 2023/24	**132-564**
Highest-rated horse in training	**Bravemansgame & Stage Star** TR c164

Chaser: Ginny's Destiny (c158): "It is hard to choose out of everything we have but Ginny was very progressive last year, winning three on the bounce at Cheltenham then finishing second at the Festival and at Aintree. I think there is loads to come from him yet."

Hurdler: Blueking d'Oroux (h152): "He was a progressive four-year-old last year and will be an ideal type to run in those good staying three-mile hurdles. Being only five there should be plenty of improvement to come."

Novice: Regent's Stroll (b108) and **Captain Teague (h140)**: "Regent's Stroll was unbeaten in two bumpers last year at Ascot and Newbury. We will hopefully follow the same route we have done with similar types of horses in the past and get some experience before going for the Challow Hurdle at Newbury over Christmas. Captain Teague was progressive in winning the Persian War and Challow Hurdle last year. He has had a wind op over the summer and I am sure there is more to come from him over fences."

Jonjo And AJ O'Neill

Wins-Runs in Britain in 2023/24	**72-505**
Highest-rated horse in training	**Monbeg Genius** Timeform Rating c145

Chaser: Monbeg Genius (c145): "Will take a similar route as last year but maybe a bit more successfully to hopefully have a go at the National."

Hurdler: Anyharminasking (h134): "He will be aimed at plenty of the big handicap hurdles this season and it would be nice to pick one of them up."

Novice: Bill Joyce (b101): "Won two bumpers last season and we saw enough to hope that he would be exciting over hurdles."

Ben Pauling

Wins-Runs in Britain in 2023/24	**76-438**
Highest-rated horse in training	**Shakem Up'Arry** Timeform Rating c149

Chaser: Bowtogreatness (c129): "He is a third-season novice chaser but has run well in big handicaps and I just can't help but feel that he still has a lot to offer and could be winning some big handicaps this season."

The Jukebox Man led up the Cheltenham hill but was overhauled close home

Hurdler: Fiercely Proud (h128): "A decent novice last season who was placed in a couple of Grade 2s. He should be very competitive in some of the decent handicap hurdles early in the season and then we can plan from there."

Novice: The Jukebox Man (h147): "A smart novice hurdler last season and he will only improve for a fence. A drop back to two and a half miles to start the season I see as a bonus, and I think he could be one of the standout novice chasers this season."

David Pipe

Wins-Runs in Britain in 2023/24	**46-385**
Highest-rated horse in training	**Gericault Roque** Timeform Rating c141

Chaser: Gericault Roque (c141): "Has been off the track for nearly two years but is still only an eight-year-old and was last seen finishing third in the Coral Gold Cup at Newbury. Shows he retains all his ability and enthusiasm at home and we can't wait to get him back on the racecourse."

Hurdler: Thomas Mor (h138): "Missed last season through injury but has some very good form in the book. He was the winner of three hurdle races and was then sixth in the Albert Bartlett at the 2023 Cheltenham Festival. Still only seven years old, he will start over hurdles but is likely to go novice chasing at some point as well. He doesn't like the ground too soft."

Novice: Jurancon (b105): "A winner of two bumpers last season and was also runner-up at Newbury. He is a very exciting prospect for novice hurdling this season. Has lots of ability and a great attitude and has schooled well at home. He will start off over two miles but likely to want further in time."

Dan Skelton

Wins-Runs in Britain in 2023/24	**120-783**
Highest-rated horse in training	**Protektorat** Timeform Rating c168

Chaser: L'Eau du Sud (h141): "He ran really well in two big handicaps last season over hurdles and he looks to be a chaser in the making."

Hurdler: Langer Dan (h156): "I think he could improve again with the step up to three miles. He's won the last two Coral Cups and ran well in graded races in the spring. He is definitely better in the spring but I think he could improve stepping up to three miles."

Novice: Royal Infantry (b105), The New Lion (b97p) and Sunray Shadow (b93p): "We have a heap of bumper winners from last season and it would be hard to split the likes of Royal Infantry, The New Lion and Sunray Shadow. They're really nice horses, we're really lucky with them and hopefully a couple could be graded material."

Langer Dan (blue and yellow) jumps the last on his way to winning a second Coral Cup

RISING STARS

Robbie Llewellyn

Base	**Overtown Farm, Wroughton, Swindon, Wiltshire**
First Full Licence	**2022**
First winner under Rules	**Tanit River** Southwell 25/05/2021
Total Winners	**34**
Best Horse Trained	**Loup de Maulde** Timeform Rating c131

In many ways Robbie Llewellyn has taken a very standard route to becoming a racehorse trainer—from starting out in pony racing as a youngster to riding in point-to-points and then becoming assistant trainer before taking out his own licence, something he did in October 2022. Less conventionally, Llewellyn also found his way into the film industry which, as has been widely reported, led to a role on horseback in Game of Thrones, but while his work as an extra was just a way of making some money, it resulted in a side-line to his increasingly successful training career as he provides racehorses for film and television work.

Training was always his long-term ambition, though, and after riding work for local Welsh trainers Tim Vaughan and Evan Williams, Llewellyn spent five years as assistant to David Brace, training his pointers during a time when Brace was twice champion owner in that sphere. After his stint outside racing, Llewellyn returned to Tim Vaughan's yard as assistant for two more years before deciding during Covid to take out his own licence.

Llewellyn's first winner under Rules in his own name had actually come before then when pointer Tanit River, formerly with Vaughan, won a hunter chase at Southwell in May 2021. However, his first winner as a full licence holder at his Wiltshire base near Alan King came in November of the following year when Loup de Maulde gained a first career success in a conditional jockeys' handicap hurdle at Huntingdon. The same horse has been as good an advertisement as any for his trainer as Loup de Maulde has improved considerably since, winning another five races to date, including his first two starts over fences in the spring of 2024. Loup de Maulde provided four of Llewellyn's five wins in his first season but 2023/24 was the stable's breakthrough campaign with a total of 25 winners gained at an impressive 23% strike rate.

Feel The Pinch, who won his first start after joining the yard, has racked up five wins for Llewellyn, while two more success stories, the hurdlers Titan Discovery and Top Cloud (another who'd won on his stable debut), provided the season's highlight when winning handicaps on consecutive days at Ascot's pre-Christmas meeting under Liam Harrison who, along with Toby Wynne, has ridden the majority of the stable's winners.

Harry Derham

Base	**Upper House Farm, Boxford, Newbury, Berkshire**
First Full Licence	**2022**
First winner under Rules	**Seelotmorebusiness** Huntingdon 26/12/2022
Total Winners	**64**
Best Horse Trained	**Brentford Hope** h149, **Fidelio Vallis** c149

Apart from being the home of numerous good horses, Ditcheat is fast becoming an academy for future trainers too and the latest of Paul Nicholls' graduates to make a success in the training ranks is Harry Derham, following the example of Nicholls' previous assistants Dan Skelton and Harry Fry. Derham has close family ties to Ditcheat too, being Nicholls' nephew, and his first job with the yard was as an amateur jockey before turning conditional. His 50 winners in the saddle—he retired from race riding when still in his teens—included a Festival success on Salubrious in the Martin Pipe Conditional Jockeys' Handicap Hurdle, though he nominates his win on Brampour in the Greatwood Hurdle at the same track, when still an amateur, as his most memorable victory as a jockey.

After six years as Nicholls' assistant, Derham began training from his purpose-built yard near Newbury late in 2022, assisted by former trainer Oliver Sherwood, and made a dream start to his new career when his very first runner, Seelotmorebusiness, formerly trained by Nicholls and carrying the colours of Derham's mother Julie, defied an absence of more than 12 months to win a handicap hurdle at Huntingdon on Boxing Day. By the end of his first season, Derham had notched 14 wins at an excellent strike rate of 25% and that one-in-four success rate was maintained in 2023/24 from a lot more runners, resulting in a much-improved total of 44 wins.

Two more ex-Nicholls horses, the chasers Sir Psycho and Fidelio Vallis, were among the leading lights for the yard last season and the latter's win under conditional Alice Stevens in quite a valuable handicap at Musselburgh formed part of a New Year's Day treble for the yard in a red-hot spell of form which yielded eight winners in all between Boxing Day and January 1. Derham's highest earner last season was Brentford Hope who'd been smart on the Flat for Richard Hughes and has now reached a similar standard over hurdles for his current yard. He has now won five times since joining Derham, including a final of the 'Challenger' series at Haydock in the spring, and has been placed in three of his other four starts, notably when runner-up in a handicap at the Punchestown Festival. The majority of Derham's winners have been ridden by stable jockey Paul O'Brien, while Stevens was appointed official second jockey prior to the start of the current season.

Jake Coen

Attached Stable	**Gordon Elliott**
First Ride	**2021 (Flat), 2023 (Jumps)**
First Winner	**Dare To Flare** Naas 22/8/2021
Total Winners	**53 (46 on Flat)**
Best Jumps Horses Ridden	**By Your Side** Timeform Rating h126

Still in his teens, Jake Coen has ridden nearly 50 winners on the Flat but that's evidently been something of a bonus because he always saw his longer-term future over jumps and, with his weight rising, decided to switch codes last summer. Coen is the younger brother of Ben, stable jockey to Johnny Murtagh and who in 2021 partnered that yard's Sonnyboyliston to win both the Ebor and Irish St Leger. The day after his elder brother gained his big win at York, Jake Coen's very first ride was a winning one when successful on 20/1 shot Dare To Flare, trained by his uncle Andrew Slattery, in an apprentices' handicap at Naas.

Later in the year, Coen made the most of plenty of opportunities on the all-weather at Dundalk, notching a couple of doubles, and ended 2021 with 11 winners. That tally more than doubled to 25 in 2022 when seven of those wins came for his boss Joseph O'Brien, though he rode winners for a dozen different trainers in all. Three of those wins came on the sprint handicapper Craft Irish and another two, including a valuable premier handicap at Cork, on Lord Dudley, while two more of his victories were gained in competitive handicaps at the Galway Festival.

In 2023, Coen went close to landing the Irish Cesarewitch on Dermot Weld's smart stayer Falcon Eight, who was runner-up at 40/1, but by then he'd already had his first rides over jumps and gained his first win in that sphere when partnering Denise Foster's Petit Dejeuner to success in a handicap hurdle at Limerick in November. While it was some time before Coen was able to add to that victory, six more wins in the early months of the current season split between Peter Fahey and Gordon Elliott point to further success to come. Attached to Elliott since switching to the jumps, Coen should have plenty more winning opportunities and has already had a couple of rides for his new yard at the Cheltenham Festival, including in the County Hurdle on By Your Side who'd been runner-up under Coen earlier in the season in a valuable handicap at Fairyhouse and at Leopardstown's Christmas meeting.

Freddie Gingell

Attached Stable	**Paul Nicholls**
First Ride	**2022**
First Winner	**West Approach** Wincanton 3/2/22
Total Winners	**47**
Best Jumps Horses Ridden	**Elixir de Nutz** Timeform Rating c158

After riding more than 50 winners on the pony racing circuit, things began to happen quickly for the then 16-year-old Freddie Gingell in the early months of 2022. Shortly after he had ridden his first winner on just his second start in point-to-points, he also won on just his second ride under Rules. That came in a two-runner hunter chase at Wincanton on West Approach, trained by his now-retired grandfather Colin Tizzard, while his next ride was a successful one, too, on the same stable's Lanspark in a handicap hurdle at Plumpton.

Gingell still had just the two winners under Rules to his name when having his first ride for Paul Nicholls only a few months later. His first win for the Ditcheat stable, on Halo des Obeaux, came at Sandown in the autumn and seven of Gingell's 11 winners in the 2022/23 season were for Nicholls. His 7 lb claim also secured him rides in some big handicaps, as he partnered Lostintranslation in the Coral Gold Cup for his uncle Joe Tizzard and Truckers Lodge in the Welsh Grand National for Nicholls.

But it was last season that Gingell's career really began to gather momentum as he notched 27 more wins largely thanks to the Tizzard and Nicholls yards. It was on Tizzard's very smart two-mile chaser Elixir de Nutz that Gingell gained his first big win in the Haldon Gold Cup at Exeter before the pair followed up in another handicap at Newbury on Coral Gold Cup day. The partnership was also maintained when Elixir de Nutz contested Grade 1 chases later in the season, even though Gingell couldn't use his claim, and was rewarded with a first win at Cheltenham when Elixir de Nutz pulled off a shock win over an out-of-sorts Jonbon in the Clarence House Chase. Truckers Lodge became another of his regular mounts and provided him with another big win in the London National at Sandown. An early highlight for Gingell in the current season came when he rode his first double which came at Plumpton in May.

ANTE-POST BETTING

Timeform's Andrew Asquith looks at the markets for some of the highlights in the National Hunt calendar and picks out his best value bets...

King George VI Chase

Hewick was a surprise winner of the King George last season, beating the likes of **Bravemansgame** and **Allaho**, but he ran a cracker on his only subsequent start over fences to finish third to **Fastorslow** and **Galopin des Champs** in the Punchestown Gold Cup. Whether he will be able to retain his King George crown in December is debateable, though, especially with some promising young chasers coming through the ranks.

Fact To File strikes as more of a Gold Cup sort, whereas **Il Est Francais** is all over a King George type. He was a very smart hurdler and quickly reached a similar level

Il Est Francais created a sparkling impression in the Kauto Star Novices' Chase

over fences last season, winning his first three starts in this sphere, notably the Kauto Star Novices' Chase over the same course and distance as the King George. Ironically, there were shades of Kauto Star in his performance that day as he displayed a high cruising speed and produced some superb leaps. Il Est Francais looked a chaser out of the top drawer and the excellent timefigure he recorded gives that form substance. Admittedly, he was disappointing on his final start at Auteuil in April, though he still looked to be going best approaching two out before finding a lot less than seemed likely. His jockey reported that he thought the horse suffered a physical problem, but nothing came to light when Il Est Francais underwent a series of tests afterwards. Connections have been easy on him since and hopefully he will reap the benefits of that in the long term.

SELECTION: Il Est Francais (6/1)

Champion Hurdle

State Man did this column a good turn when winning the Champion Hurdle last season (advised by John Ingles at 8/1), but he is a general 4/1 to retain his crown at the time of writing and that doesn't make much appeal given it has the potential to be a much deeper renewal. **Lossiemouth** is a very interesting contender given she won the Mares' Hurdle in a manner that underlines she'd have been a big threat to State Man had she run in the Champion Hurdle. Connections won the race with another mare in Annie Power in 2016 and Lossiemouth certainly has all the tools to make her of firm interest.

However, there is the not-so-small matter of **Constitution Hill** to consider. The 2023 Champion Hurdle winner had a truncated campaign last season, not getting the chance to defend his crown due to a respiratory infection, but there is little doubt that he's the top hurdler around when he's on song. In fact, he established himself as potentially the best hurdler of all time when trouncing Jonbon by 22 lengths in the Supreme Novices' Hurdle in 2022, producing the best performance by a novice hurdler in Timeform's experience. He hasn't needed to repeat that effort in winning five Grade 1s in open company since, but he certainly has the ability to do so when the occasion demands it. Constitution Hill has only been available to back at odds against on two occasions in his career, on his debut and in the Supreme, so a top-price 5/2 for this season's Champion Hurdle looks very attractive indeed. Reports coming out of Seven Barrows are positive, with Nicky Henderson recently stating, 'I've never seen him look so well'. He will likely return in the Fighting Fifth and a smooth victory there will see his price contract, so the advice is to get Constitution Hill on side now at what may turn out to be a massive price.

SELECTION: Constitution Hill (5/2)

Queen Mother Champion Chase

Energumene, the 2022 and 2023 winner of the Champion Chase, was ruled out of last season through injury, but he is set to return to racing this campaign and connections will surely be seeking to win this race for a third time with him. He will be an 11-year-old, though, and will be competing with some up-and-coming chasers. **El Fabiolo** was turned over as the 9/2-on favourite in last season's renewal and his tendency to throw in a clanger at his fences means he is a risky proposition. Impressive Arkle winner **Gaelic Warrior** has to come into the conversation, but he is versatile trip-wise and is also a possibility for the Ryanair, so is difficult to back with confidence this far out.

The forgotten horse—at least where the market is concerned—is **Marine Nationale**, who won his first six starts under Rules, notably the Supreme Novices' Hurdle, and he looked destined for the top when making a winning start over fences at Leopardstown in December last year. That was a near-flawless transition to chasing by Marine Nationale who was very nimble at his fences and proved in a different league to his rivals at every stage of the race, recording an excellent timefigure in the process.

Marine Nationale was disappointing up in grade when beaten by **Il Etait Temps** in the Irish Arkle Novice Chase at the Dublin Racing Festival, but he clearly wasn't right that day and he hasn't been seen since as he was ruled out of the Arkle after suffering

Marine Nationale impressed on his chasing debut and has more to offer over fences

a suspensory strain. It's possible that Marine Nationale could be seen on the Flat this autumn, according to his trainer, but his main target is the Champion Chase and he remains a very exciting prospect. Marine Nationale is around 14/1 and it's hard not to think he'll be much shorter than that with a clear path to Cheltenham.

SELECTION: Marine Nationale (14/1)

Stayers' Hurdle

Teahupoo announced himself as the best around in the staying hurdling division last season, winning all three starts, including this contest from **Flooring Porter** and **Home By The Lee** to gain compensation for when he had experienced a less-than-ideal passage in third a year earlier. He had started the season by winning the Hatton's Grace Hurdle at Fairyhouse and completed a perfect campaign in comfortable fashion in the Champion Stayers Hurdle at Punchestown in May, and he will likely follow a similar path to Cheltenham this season as he is seemingly at his best when fresh.

Teahupoo is a worthy favourite, but, at a bigger price, **Theleme** looks a fascinating contender. He is a prolific winner in France and has been successful on six of his last seven starts, including the Grand Prix d'Automne which he won for the second successive year when last seen in November. He didn't need to be at his best on that occasion, but he still won very easily, displaying a smart turn of foot to quicken clear on the run-in. He was reportedly being aimed at the Stayers' Hurdle at Cheltenham but suffered a setback in January which ruled him out. However, the plan is to try again this season. Theleme (173) is rated 10 lb higher than Teahupoo on Timeform ratings and was as short as 4/1 when ruled out of Cheltenham so, given it wasn't a major injury, he looks fairly priced at around 8/1 and is worth getting on side.

SELECTION: Theleme (8/1)

Cheltenham Gold Cup

Galopin des Champs put up one of the best performances in the Gold Cup in recent years when winning in 2023 and he ran to a similar level when retaining his crown in March. He did so under contrasting conditions, too, having no problem with the much more testing ground and finding plenty in the closing stages to beat **Gerri Colombe** by three and a half lengths. Galopin des Champs is unbeaten in three completed starts at Cheltenham and he would have comfortably won the Turners Novices' Chase in 2022 had he not fallen at the last. He looks a worthy favourite in his pursuit of winning the race three years in a row.

Stablemate **Fact To File** isn't far behind him in the betting and he looks very intriguing indeed. Willie Mullins made the unusual decision to skip hurdling with him, but it paid dividends as he finished the season as the second highest-rated novice chaser behind

Fastorslow is a top-class staying chaser

only Gaelic Warrior, who he beat in a match at Leopardstown prior to winning the Brown Advisory Novices' Chase at the Cheltenham Festival. He seems sure to make his mark in open company this season and remains a most exciting prospect, but, at the prices, it is **Fastorslow** who looks the bet at this stage. Fastorslow has beaten Galopin des Champs three times (all at Punchestown), including in the Punchestown Gold Cup on his latest start. Fastorslow clearly goes well at Punchestown, but his record at Cheltenham isn't a bad one, either, for all he's yet to win. He finished runner-up in the Coral Cup and Ultima Handicap Chase (to subsequent Grand National winner Corach Rambler), and he was still going well when unseating his rider in the Gold Cup last season. Whether he should be three times the price of Galopin des Champs is questionable. Fastorslow is still relatively lightly raced and, with just eight starts over fences in Britain or Ireland, he may have even more to offer.

SELECTION: Fastorslow (12/1)

Grand National

I Am Maximus developed into a top-class chaser last season, making a winning return in the Grade 1 Drinmore Novice Chase at Fairyhouse and ending his campaign with a victory in the Grand National. He is the ante-post favourite to win again next year, but he will face a much stiffer task following a rise in the weights.

Interestingly, I Am Maximus won the Irish Grand National in his previous season, and it is the most recent winner of that race, **Intense Raffles**, who makes most appeal for the Grand National at this stage. He's a lightly-raced six-year-old who was unbeaten over hurdles in France and he has won all three of his starts over fences for these connections. Each time he took a big step forward in form terms, but, perhaps more impressively, he also took the transition from small-field novice events to a large-field, competitive handicap in his stride when completing a hat-trick in the Irish Grand National at Fairyhouse. That was his handicap debut and Intense Raffles moved through that race like a horse on a very good mark, while he also found plenty for pressure over a longer trip to see off the strong-staying Any Second Now, who isn't getting any younger but has an excellent Grand National record. Intense Raffles jumped well on his first two starts in Ireland in less-competitive races, but it was encouraging that he only really made one mistake in the Irish Grand National. That bodes well for one so inexperienced as a chaser, while he clearly stays well, so he has the right sort of profile to develop into a Grand National candidate next year. The general 25/1 on offer looks fair for one who has yet to reach the ceiling of his ability.

SELECTIONS: Intense Raffles (25/1)

The progressive Intense Raffles looks a suitable candidate for the Grand National

SECTION 4

TIMEFORM'S VIEW

Chosen from the Timeform formbook, here is Timeform's detailed analysis— compiled by our team of race reporters—of a selection of key races from Cheltenham.

CHELTENHAM Tuesday March 12

HEAVY

Sky Bet Supreme Novices' Hurdle (Grade 1) (1)

Pos	*Btn*	*Horse*	*Age*	*Wgt*	*Eq*	*Trainer*	*Jockey*	*SP*
1		SLADE STEEL (IRE)	6	11-7	(t)	Henry de Bromhead, Ireland	Rachael Blackmore	7/2
2	1½	MYSTICAL POWER (IRE)	5	11-7	(h)	W. P. Mullins, Ireland	M. P. Walsh	10/3
3	3½	FIREFOX (IRE)	6	11-7		Gordon Elliott, Ireland	J. W. Kennedy	11/2
4	nk	ASIAN MASTER (IRE)	7	11-7		W. P. Mullins, Ireland	T. R. Costello	16/1
5	2¼	MISTERGIF (FR)	5	11-7	(h)	W. P. Mullins, Ireland	Daryl Jacob	18/1
6	2¼	FAVOUR AND FORTUNE (IRE)	6	11-7		Alan King	Tom Cannon	28/1
7	½	SUPERSUNDAE (FR)	5	11-7		W. P. Mullins, Ireland	Mr P. W. Mullins	66/1
8	2¼	TULLYHILL (FR)	6	11-7	(t)	W. P. Mullins, Ireland	P. Townend	11/4f
9	3	KINGS HILL (IRE)	5	11-7		Paul John Gilligan, Ireland	Jack G. Gilligan	150/1
10	nk	TELLHERTHENAME (IRE)	5	11-7		Ben Pauling	Kielan Woods	14/1
pu		JERIKO DU REPONET (FR)	5	11-7		Nicky Henderson	Nico de Boinville	11/1

11 ran Race Time 4m 13.80 Closing Sectional (4.10f): 61.4s (103.3%) Winning Owner: Robcour

Significant overnight rain meant the first day of the Festival started on unusually testing ground, which certainly had an impact on the way this race was run, the field still well grouped 2 out, potentially one or 2 of the longer-priced runners flattered by the way it unfolded; the race had quite an open look to it beforehand, with the leading novice of the season Ballyburn instead going for the Baring Bingham, his form franked by the winner who'd been runner-up to him in the Brave Inca, the race totally dominated by Irish stables, the British managing just 3 runners, the form probably a bit below standard for the race, only Summerville Boy obviously inferior among the winners in the last decade. **Slade Steel** held leading claims in the absence of Ballyburn and progressed again, doing well to recover from fluffing the last, though in a better position than most the way the race developed; close up, took keen hold, led early in straight, shaken up soon after, untidy last and headed, rallied well, led again final 100 yds, driven clear; open to further improvement. **Mystical Power** progressed again in first-time hood, not having such a good run through as the winner but getting to the front late on only to be done by a stronger stayer; held up, short of room 2 out, headway straight, chased leaders approaching last, jumped on there, headed final 100 yds, outstayed; an athletic sort, the type go on improving. **Firefox** showed improved form this time, even though he wasn't seen to best advantage, sure to have got closer still in a more truly-run race and with more luck in running; held up, smooth headway 3 out, shaken up straight and short of room, not quicken, kept on run-in; very much a chaser on looks, he seems sure to go on to better things. **Asian Master** ran well, though he left the impression he had an even better effort in him, his regular amateur rider unable to claim and rather caught out when the race developed into the straight; in touch, headway approaching 3 out, loomed up after next, not quicken before last, stayed on run-in; he has the build of a chaser for next season. **Mistergif** ran well upped in grade, though couldn't sustain the effort having got himself into a place soon after the last; held up, effort 2 out, chased leaders approaching last, no extra run-in; he has more about him than might be expected from his pedigree and he could well make at least as good a novice over fences next season. **Favour And Fortune** emerged best of the paltry home team, running as well as he has, that he ran a race at all quite surprising given he nearly lost his rider at the first; held up, bad mistake first, not fluent fourth, pushed along 3 out, some headway approaching last, one paced. **Supersundae** on first outing since leaving Anne-Sophie Pacault after 11 months off, seemed to improve plenty on his 2 efforts in France, that his stable saw fit to run him in this reason enough to give him credit for now; held up, ridden when mistake 2 out, kept on run-in, never on terms. **Tullyhill** looked the pick of his stable's 5 runners but failed to meet expectations, his finish to the race rather tame; led, took keen hold, headed third, led again 3 out, shaken up straight and headed, weakening when mistake last; despite this reverse, he's a smart prospect for novice chasing next season. **Kings Hill** seemed to excel himself up considerably in grade but did beat only one home; in touch, tracked pace 2 out, left behind quickly home turn. **Tellherthename** had plenty on in this grade; disputed lead, went on third, headed early in straight, weakened approaching last; he ought to make a useful novice chaser next winter. **Jeriko du Reponet** ran no sort of race, the first of several poor efforts from his stable's runners on the afternoon, something likely to be not right, his overall profile suggesting he's best forgiven this run; in touch, mistake first, not fluent third, pushed along after fifth, weakened 2 out, pulled up last.

My Pension Expert Arkle Challenge Trophy Novices' Chase (Grade 1) (1)

Pos	Btn	Horse	Age	Wgt	Eq	Trainer	Jockey	SP
1		GAELIC WARRIOR (GER)	6	11-7	(h)	W. P. Mullins, Ireland	P. Townend	2/1f
2	8½	FOUND A FIFTY (IRE)	7	11-7		Gordon Elliott, Ireland	J. W. Kennedy	13/2
3	4¾	IL ETAIT TEMPS (FR)	6	11-7	(h+t)	W. P. Mullins, Ireland	D. E. Mullins	7/2
4	6	MATATA (IRE)	6	11-7		Nigel Twiston-Davies	Sam Twiston-Davies	22/1
5	2¼	HUNTERS YARN (IRE)	7	11-7		W. P. Mullins, Ireland	Daryl Jacob	15/2
6	9½	MY MATE MOZZIE (IRE)	8	11-7	(s+t)	Gavin Patrick Cromwell, Ireland	Keith Donoghue	25/1
7	3	JPR ONE (IRE)	7	11-7		Joe Tizzard	Brendan Powell	16/1
8	5	QUILIXIOS	7	11-7		Henry de Bromhead, Ireland	Rachael Blackmore	11/2
F		AUTHORISED SPEED (FR)	7	11-7		Gary Moore	David Noonan	100/1
F		MASTER CHEWY (IRE)	7	11-7		Nigel Twiston-Davies	Tom Bellamy	22/1

10 ran Race Time 4m 08.90 Closing Sectional (3.75f): 57.6s (101.9%) Winning Owner: Mrs S. Ricci

An Arkle that provided a snapshot of the current state of jump racing, the first 5 in the market trained in Ireland and numbering 3 Grade 1 winners over fences among them, the 4 British-trained runners sent off at 16/1 or bigger, the best of their victories coming at Grade 2 level, the Irish dominating the finish, even though a couple of the fancied runners failed to fire and another made 2 significant mistakes; the pace was a fair one, picking up 3 out, a handy position perhaps an advantage, though the first 2, close up at that point, were surely the 2 best in the race anyway, the winner's performance well up to standard for the race, if not quite matching the most illustrious of his stable's winners of the race. **Gaelic Warrior** runner-up at this meeting twice as a hurdler, including in last season's Baring Bingham, quickly got back on the up over fences after his flop at Leopardstown, coping well with the drop to 2m (under testing conditions), his jumping passing the test with no issue going left handed, his performance overall in a first-time hood a polished one, even if his edgy demeanour beforehand had been a bit of a concern; tracked pace, tanked along, loomed up early in straight, led approaching last, quickened clear run-in, had bit in hand; he may well have more to offer and, given his effectiveness over further, will have plenty of options out of novice company next season. **Found A Fifty** highly tried and not up to this level as a novice hurdler, is much more a chaser on looks and he's built an excellent record this season, a winner once and second 3 times in Grade 1s, clearly effective at 2m, though his optimum trip likely to prove over further, the Manifesto at Aintree perhaps an option for adding a second notable victory; prominent, travelled well, upsides 3 out, went on before 2 out, ridden soon after, headed approaching last, left behind by winner run-in. **Il Etait Temps** a gutsy winner over the runner-up last time, wasn't disgraced, though a couple of significant mistakes cost him his chance of making more of an impact, no surprise if he proves more competitive at Punchestown; held up, mistake eighth, bad mistake tenth, ridden 3 out, not quicken, stayed on straight, took third run-in. **Matata** wasn't disgraced, his exertions telling late on after he'd set the pace for a superior pair; led, shaken up after 3 out, headed straight, weakened after 2 out. **Hunters Yarn** had run to a high level when winning a maiden at Fairyhouse last time, but the huge step up in class proved a bit much at this early stage of his chasing career, never threatening to get involved; held up, mistake first, effort 3 out, hung right, hampered 2 out, made no impression; he's a fine stamp of a chaser and may yet make his mark at a good level. **My Mate Mozzie** the oldest in the field and about the least taking physically, was below form after 11 weeks off, the ground having turned against him; held up, mistake ninth, shaken up 3 out, made no impression. **Jpr One** had something to find against the pick of the Irish-trained runners but came up a long way short even so, as in the Henry VIII not finishing his race so well as seemed likely from the way he travelled; waited with, shaken up after 3 out, hampered 2 out, weakened run-in. **Quilixios** had made a good start over fences but ran no sort of race after 2 months off, perhaps something amiss, though nothing came to light immediately; patiently ridden, not settle fully, effort briefly 3 out, no response. **Authorised Speed** looked an optimistic runner at this level and didn't get the chance to disprove that; mid-division, fell second. **Master Chewy** was set to run at least respectably when he came down, likely to have finished in front of the fourth; held up, headway 3 out, keeping on when fell 2 out; he should have a future as a smart 2m handicapper next season.

Unibet Champion Hurdle Challenge Trophy (Grade 1) (1)

Pos	*Btn*	*Horse*	*Age*	*Wgt*	*Eq*	*Trainer*	*Jockey*	*SP*
1		STATE MAN (FR)	7	11-10		W. P. Mullins, Ireland	P. Townend	2/5f
2	1¼	IRISH POINT (FR)	6	11-10		Gordon Elliott, Ireland	J. W. Kennedy	9/2
3	2¼	LUCCIA	6	11-3		Nicky Henderson	James Bowen	33/1
4	6	ZARAK THE BRAVE (FR)	5	11-10		W. P. Mullins, Ireland	Daryl Jacob	22/1
5	1½	COLONEL MUSTARD (FR)	9	11-10	(b)	Mrs Lorna Fowler, Ireland	J. J. Slevin	50/1
6	6½	NEMEAN LION (GER)	7	11-10		Kerry Lee	Richard Patrick	12/1
7	37	NOT SO SLEEPY	12	11-10		Hughie Morrison	Sean Bowen	33/1
pu		IBERICO LORD (FR)	6	11-10		Nicky Henderson	Nico de Boinville	11/1

8 ran Race Time 4m 14.40 Closing Sectional (4.10f): 60.2s (105.6%) Winning Owner: Mrs J. Donnelly

The first Champion Hurdle run on heavy ground since the 'eighties, the time as slow as any for the race since the course was changed in 1980 and slower than for the Supreme earlier on the card, this race run at a pretty steady pace, the field still closely bunched 2 out; most of the talk beforehand was about the outstanding Constitution Hill, last season's stunning winner who was forced to miss the race this time due to not being right, the impressive International Hurdle winner Lossiemouth—who won the Mares' Hurdle 40 minutes later—and the Baring

Bingham winner Impaire Et Passe other notable absentees, the field on the day woefully short on depth, last season's runner-up State Man sent off at very short odds, his main market rival rerouted from the Stayers'; things proved pretty straightforward for the favourite—the fifth successive market leader to win the Champion—and he didn't have to run quite to his best to prevail, the proximity of Luccia and Colonel Mustard giving reason to take a relatively low view of the form. **State Man** added yet another Grade 1 to his tally without having to run quite to his best, his task made much easier by the absence of Constitution Hill; never far away, travelled smoothly, loomed up entering straight, led last, shaken up run-in, asserted; he's got a tremendous record, though he's helped by the dearth of good 2m hurdlers on both sides of the Irish Sea. **Irish Point** rerouted from the Stayers' Hurdle after the defection of Constitution Hill, ran well, just lacking the pace of the winner late on, this just his third start of the campaign, every chance he'll turn up at Aintree (won the Mersey there last season), with a choice of the Aintree or Liverpool Hurdle, the decision perhaps again resting on whether Constitution Hill is back on the scene; handy, travelled well, went on entering straight, shaken up soon after and joined, headed last, not quicken. **Luccia** after 3 months off, seemed to excel herself up in grade, the one bright spot on the afternoon for her yard, most of which's fancied runners were pulled up before the last; soon steadied, not settle fully, shaken up after 2 out, chased leaders last, kept on; she has limited options for the rest of the season, and it may be that the paddocks beckon. **Zarak The Brave** ran creditably up in grade, though only briefly looking a threat in the straight; held up, pushed along after fifth, chased leaders approaching last, not quicken run-in; he's not an obvious chaser on looks, likely to prove a bits-and-pieces player in good hurdle races next season. **Colonel Mustard** in first-time blinkers (tried in cheekpieces previously), ran as well as he can upped in grade, though never in with much of a shout; soon steadied (close up first), outpaced after 2 out, kept on run-in. **Nemean Lion** up still further in grade, found his progress coming to a halt, essentially finding the company too hot; led first, tracked pace after, not fluent third, fifth, led 3 out, shaken up after 2 out, headed, weakened straight. **Not So Sleepy** making his fifth appearance in the Champion Hurdle, returning from 3 months off, was well held, as he had been last season; raced very freely, led after first, not fluent fourth, ridden when headed and mistake 3 out, weakened quickly 2 out. **Iberico Lord** supplemented for the race, looked an interesting runner at this level, but his yard is having plenty run badly at the moment and he was another, clearly just not himself, likely to be worth another chance at pattern level when his stable is back on song; held up, shaken up before 3 out, dropped away 2 out, pulled up last; he's the look of a chaser and ought to be one to follow over fences next season, this surely just a blip.

Close Brothers Mares' Hurdle (David Nicholson) (Grade 1) (1)

Pos	*Btn*	*Horse*	*Age*	*Wgt*	*Eq*	*Trainer*	*Jockey*	*SP*
1		LOSSIEMOUTH (FR)	5	11-5		W. P. Mullins, Ireland	P. Townend	8/13f
2	3	TELMESOMETHINGGIRL (IRE)	9	11-5		Henry de Bromhead, Ireland	Rachael Blackmore	22/1
3	9½	HISPANIC MOON (FR)	7	11-5		Henry de Bromhead, Ireland	D. J. O'Keeffe	40/1
4	sh	LANTRY LADY (FR)	6	11-5	(t)	Henry de Bromhead, Ireland	J. W. Kennedy	18/1
5	1¼	LOVE ENVOI (IRE)	8	11-5	(s+t)	Harry Fry	Jonathan Burke	14/1
6	15	GALA MARCEAU (FR)	5	11-5	(h)	W. P. Mullins, Ireland	D. E. Mullins	12/1
7	18	YOU WEAR IT WELL	7	11-5		Jamie Snowden	Gavin Sheehan	25/1
pu		ASHROE DIAMOND (IRE)	7	11-5	(h)	W. P. Mullins, Ireland	Mr P. W. Mullins	15/2
pu		ECHOES IN RAIN (FR)	8	11-5	(h+t)	W. P. Mullins, Ireland	B. Hayes	14/1

pu		MARIE'S ROCK (IRE)	9	11-5	(t)	Nicky Henderson	Nico de Boinville	12/1
pu		THEATRE GLORY (IRE)	7	11-5	(s)	Nicky Henderson	James Bowen	125/1

11 ran Race Time 5m 11.10 Closing Sectional (4.10f): 61.4s (104.3%) Winning Owner: Mrs S. Ricci

A lop-sided betting market mirrored what happened in a race that saw Lossiemouth produce the best winning performance since Honeysuckle's first success in 2020, the way she did it—cruising through from out the back in a race run at no more than a fair gallop—raising hope that she can go some way to emulating the storied exploits of that great mare in open company. **Lossiemouth** outclassed a field of mares in a manner that underlines she'd have been the main threat to State Man had she instead contested the Champion Hurdle, that race on the agenda for next season with little doubt she's got the all the tools required to win open Grade 1s; held up, jumped well, smooth headway from 4 out, produced between rivals early in straight, jumped on last, quickened clear, the longer trip no problem at all. **Telmesomethinggirl** looked back to her very best, beating the rest decisively and just unlucky to bump into an outstanding winner; in touch, travelled fluently, led home turn, headed last, kept on, no match for winner. **Hispanic Moon** ran well faced with a stiffer task; mid-division, ridden after 2 out, went third flat; her very best French form came over fences. **Lantry Lady** ran well considering her lack of experience and was strong at the finish, leaving the impression we still haven't seen the very best of her; dropped out, headway when not fluent 2 out, pushed along home turn, kept on well flat and nearly snatched third. **Love Envoi** in first-time cheekpieces, underperformed for the first time in 3 visits to the Festival, turning for home with every chance but faltering up the hill; raced wide, held up, headway out wide sixth, upsides 2 out, no extra before last; she's reportedly been retired. **Gala Marceau** is best not judged on this run, little going right for her; held up, not clear run after sixth, hampered again 3 out, never involved. **You Wear It Well** ran poorly; soon led, headed fourth, lost place 2 out, weakened. **Ashroe Diamond** is best not judged on this run in a first-time hood, the decision to make the running an odd one and clearly not working; prominent, took strong hold, jumped on fourth, headed 2 out, weakened quickly. **Echoes In Rain** back in a hood, unseated her rider at the start and turned in a rare poor effort, never threatening to improve from off the pace. **Marie's Rock** performed lamentably, wretched stable form the obvious reason why; mid-division, carried head bit awkwardly, mistake 4 out, weakened. **Theatre Glory** in first-time cheekpieces, faced a stiff task but ran no sort of race all the same; prominent, lost place sixth, tailed off when blundered 2 out.

Maureen Mullins National Hunt Challenge Cup Amateur Jockeys' Novices' Chase (Grade 2) (1)

Pos	*Btn*	*Horse*	*Age*	*Wgt*	*Eq*	*Trainer*	*Jockey*	*SP*
1		CORBETTS CROSS (IRE)	7	11-7	(h)	Emmet Mullins, Ireland	Mr D. O'Connor	15/8
2	17	EMBASSY GARDENS	8	11-7	(h)	W. P. Mullins, Ireland	Mr P. W. Mullins	7/4f
3	8½	MR VANGO (IRE)	8	11-7	(s)	Sara Bradstock	Miss Gina Andrews	14/1
4	6½	KILBEG KING (IRE)	9	11-7	(s+t)	Anthony Honeyball	Mr William Biddick	20/1
5	13	APPLE AWAY (IRE)	7	11-0		Lucinda Russell	Mr B. O'Neill	5/1
pu		HENRY'S FRIEND (IRE)	7	11-7	(s)	Ben Pauling	Mr Jack Andrews	33/1
pu		SALVADOR ZIGGY (IRE)	8	11-7		Gordon Elliott, Ireland	Mr R. James	10/1

7 ran Race Time 8m 26.70 Closing Sectional (3.75f): 60.4s (105.2%) Winning Owner: Mr John P. McManus

A below-average turnout for the second time in the last 3 years for a race—one of 3 restricted to amateurs across the meeting—that feels closer than any of the others at the modern-day Festival to being on borrowed time, not that the wheels tend to turn very quickly when it comes to introducing potential solutions to revive the competitiveness in some areas of the sport's figurehead fixture, a rout by Corbetts Cross of a standard that would surely have made him a big contender in the more prestigious Broadway the following day; the pace was steady yet the picture changed rapidly all the same in the straight as the market leaders made their move from rear together, contrasting finishing efforts setting them apart. **Corbetts Cross** did in a Cheltenham novice chase what had been expected of him in a novice hurdle at the meeting in 2023, making amends for that late mishap in the Albert Bartlett in a style so dominant that he'd have been able to make light of any rather more minor incidents along the way; a steady pace placed little emphasis on his jumping or stamina, but things still came very easily to him and, after cruising to the front entering the straight, he burst clear in most striking style, adding another 11 lengths to his winning margin on the run-in alone to post one of the best performances on the book in the race this century, one more becoming of a Broadway than a Grade 2 novice in truth; he ought to take on the top-level novices at the next spring festival, however, in the Mildmay at Aintree. **Embassy Gardens** went some way to putting to bed doubts over his effectiveness at this track following his blowout in the 2023 Albert Bartlett but still promised more than he delivered tried hooded, attempting to mirror the winner's move but making the worst of several errors on the way around at the second last and left for dead on the run-in, his stamina possibly stretched by then, though an irregular heartbeat did come to light. **Mr Vango** ran about as well as could have been expected upped in grade following a handicap rout from a BHA mark of just 120, the addition of cheekpieces not providing the required jolt; made running, pushed along soon after 3 out, headed entering straight, no extra 2 out, tiring when blundered last. **Kilbeg King** wasn't up to the task, like the other 2 from the Reynoldstown doing nothing for that form against a pair of Irish novices; in touch, lost place when not fluent fourteenth, shaken up before 3 out, rallied until straight, held when untidy 2 out. **Apple Away** was sent off at much shorter odds than the other 2 involved in a bunched finish to the Reynoldstown but, like that pair, ultimately failed to run near the same level, furthering a rather stop-start first season in largely good company over fences; tracked pace, pressed leader from eighth, pecked fourteenth, every chance 3 out, dropped away straight. **Henry's Friend** had his winning run ended in listless fashion, giving the firm impression Ascot had taken more out of him than it had the reopposing pair from the Reynoldstown, not that they covered themselves in much glory, either; tracked pace until halfway, not going well from sixteenth, struggling 5 out. **Salvador Ziggy** was said to have bled on his venture to America when last seen in the autumn and returned with anything but a bang, soon beaten once asked for an effort running to 3 out.

CHELTENHAM Wednesday March 13

HEAVY

Gallagher Novices' Hurdle (Baring Bingham) (Grade 1) (1)

Pos	Btn	Horse	Age	Wgt	Eq	Trainer	Jockey	SP
1		BALLYBURN (IRE)	6	11-7		W. P. Mullins, Ireland	P. Townend	1/2f
2	13	JIMMY DU SEUIL (FR)	5	11-7		W. P. Mullins, Ireland	S. F. O'Keeffe	66/1
3	3½	ILE ATLANTIQUE (FR)	6	11-7		W. P. Mullins, Ireland	Mr P. W. Mullins	9/2
4	6	MERCUREY (FR)	6	11-7		W. P. Mullins, Ireland	B. Hayes	40/1
5	3¼	PREDATORS GOLD (FR)	5	11-7		W. P. Mullins, Ireland	D. E. Mullins	7/1
6	16	HANDSTANDS (IRE)	5	11-7		Ben Pauling	Harry Cobden	20/1
pu		JINGKO BLUE (FR)	5	11-7		Nicky Henderson	Nico de Boinville	20/1

7 ran Race Time 5m 23.20 Closing Sectional (4.10f): 60.3s (104.6%) Winning Owner: R.A.Bartlett/David Manasseh

Just 7 runners, the withdrawal of a no-hoper leaving this the joint-smallest field for the Baring Bingham in its current form—dating back 50 years—after 7 had also lined-up in 2021, the field a perfect illustration of the current state of jump racing, one stable represented by 5 of the 7, British yards, seeking a first win in the race for the home team since 2017, responsible for the other 2, both 20/1 shots and pulled up/tailed off at the finish; Willie Mullins ended the first 2 days having won 6 of the 8 Grade 1 races, sending out the favourite in 7 of the 8, 5 of those at odds on, the only irony the defeat of the shortest-priced runner, such a dominance not Mullins' fault but hardly a picture of a healthy sport, that perhaps one factor in Cheltenham drawing the smallest crowd for the Wednesday of the Festival since 2009; Ballyburn stood out on form beforehand, having run to a level good enough to win an average Baring Bingham when beating the subsequent Supreme winner Slade Steel in the Brave Inca, and he scored in impressive fashion in a good overall time, his performance well up to the level shown by the best recent winners. **Ballyburn** looked potentially top class in following up his Brave Inca win in most decisive fashion, untroubled by the return to a longer trip (or anything else), his very low head carriage often thought of as a sign of a horse that will be better over fences, which would make him some chaser for next season and beyond, his physique and pedigree also suggesting that route; tracked pace, travelled powerfully, upsides 3 out, led on bridle soon after, in command straight, well clear run-in, impressive. **Jimmy du Seuil** who sweated up and was on his toes beforehand, had limited experience over hurdles, just 2 runs in maidens, but he'd shown plenty of potential and improved significantly upped in grade and over a 4f longer trip; dropped out, took keen hold, headway when not fluent, hampered 2 out, went second early in straight, kept on, no match for winner; he probably has still more to offer as a hurdler. **Ile Atlantique** was placed at Grade 1 level for the second time in just 3 starts over hurdles for Mullins, matching his effort behind Readin Tommy Wrong (running in the Spa later in the week) at Naas last time, again plenty to like about the performance of one that is every inch a chaser on looks; held up, travelled well, headway 2 out, ridden straight, one paced, mistake last. **Mercurey** a wide-margin maiden winner last time out, was upped markedly in trip and ran about as well as could have been expected upped in grade; led, shaken up after 2 out, headed soon after, lost second early in straight, weakened run-in; he's an athletic sort and, like the others in the stable's quintet, he appeals as a prospective chaser for next season. **Predators Gold** twice a runner-up at Grade 1 level, was let down by his jumping and ran below his best; held up, mistake sixth, headway when mistake 3 out, shaken up after, blundered 2 out, left behind straight; he looks the part for chasing. **Handstands** came into this unbeaten in 3 starts over hurdles, but he was stepping up significantly in class and wasn't nearly up to the task, left behind turning for home and running some way below form. **Jingko Blue** was allowed to take his chance, despite the poor performances of quite a few of his stable's runners on the first day (several others withdrawn from this card), but he was badly let down by his jumping and dropped away much as his stable-companions had the day before; in touch, mistakes third, fourth and fifth (blundered and rider lost irons), pushed along before 3 out, weakened, pulled up straight; he'd looked a smart prospect previously and will hopefully bounce back when his stable is over whatever is ailing it at the moment.

Brown Advisory Novices' Chase (Broadway) (Grade 1) (1)

Pos	Btn	Horse	Age	Wgt	Eq	Trainer	Jockey	SP
1		FACT TO FILE (FR)	7	11-7		W. P. Mullins, Ireland	M. P. Walsh	8/13f
2	3¾	MONTY'S STAR (IRE)	7	11-7		Henry de Bromhead, Ireland	Rachael Blackmore	13/2
3	2½	GIOVINCO (IRE)	7	11-7		Lucinda Russell	Stephen Mulqueen	40/1
4	3¾	SANDOR CLEGANE (IRE)	7	11-7	(t)	Paul Nolan, Ireland	S. F. O'Keeffe	16/1
5	38	AMERICAN MIKE (IRE)	7	11-7	(t)	Gordon Elliott, Ireland	J. W. Kennedy	7/1
pu		STAY AWAY FAY (IRE)	7	11-7	(s+t)	Paul Nicholls	Harry Cobden	6/1

6 ran Race Time 6m 42.40 Closing Sectional (3.75f): 56.7s (108.6%) Winning Owner: Mr John P. McManus

A smallish field for the Broadway but an up-to-scratch renewal and the winner figures among the most promising horses to have contested the race in recent seasons, such a comfortable verdict over smart rivals strong evidence that this is the very least of what he can do; the lead was disputed but it was just a fair gallop and the race really took shape only after 3 out. **Fact To File** on his toes in the paddock and with 2 handlers, hammered home his status as a chaser with Gold Cup potential as he brushed his rivals aside on his first try around 3m; held up in fifth, he took a couple of fences to warm to the task (jumped high and slightly to the right early) but was very fluent thereafter, making smooth progress into contention 3 out, challenging at the next then sealing the deal with a superb jump at the last, drawing clear on the flat for just 1 crack on the whip; he's a top-class chaser in the making and will surely be winning in open Grade 1 company next season. **Monty's Star** ran a fine race up in grade on his third outing over fences and just his seventh overall, lacking the class of the winner but showing lots of likeable qualities of his own that'll see him win good races in the seasons to come; pressed leader, jumped soundly, shaken up before 2 out, upsides there, left behind by winner soon after last, kept on. **Giovinco** excelled himself back in grade with absolutely no hint of flattery to the performance, jumping/travelling well off the pace, making smooth headway to track the leaders 3 out and keeping on well into third on the run-in having been switched off the inside turning for home; on this form, he'd have taken all the beating from a mark of 146 in the Ultima, that set to suffer now, though surely not enough to see him scooping some good prizes for a yard that's a formidable force in the top staying handicap chases. **Sandor Clegane** ran a fine race at the Festival for the second year running, showing a fair bit of improvement and losing ground on the principals only in the final 100 yds; close up, not fluent sixth, pressed leader seventh, edged ahead eleventh, pushed along home turn, headed 2 out, untidy last, no extra; it's going to be worth preserving his novice status for next season, though he's the type to go well in the top staying handicaps in seasons to come. **American Mike** underperformed, spoiling his chance with 2 bad mistakes; mid-division, blundered ninth, fourteenth, ridden after 3 out, weakened after 3 out. **Stay Away Fay** in first-time cheekpieces, proved to be a disappointment for the first time in his life, harried for the lead and giving way rather tamely (lost shoe and later scoped dirty, too), his earlier form advertised by Giovinco; led narrowly, mistake seventh, headed eleventh, shaken up approaching 3 out, weakened before next.

Betway Queen Mother Champion Chase (Grade 1) (1)

Pos	Btn	Horse	Age	Wgt	Eq	Trainer	Jockey	SP
1		CAPTAIN GUINNESS (IRE)	9	11-10		Henry de Bromhead, Ireland	Rachael Blackmore	17/2
2	1½	GENTLEMAN DE MEE (FR)	8	11-10	(h+t)	W. P. Mullins, Ireland	M. P. Walsh	16/1
3	49	FUNAMBULE SIVOLA (FR)	9	11-10		Venetia Williams	Charlie Deutsch	100/1

F		EDWARDSTONE	10	11-10		Alan King	Tom Cannon	15/2
pu		EL FABIOLO (FR)	7	11-10		W. P. Mullins, Ireland	P. Townend	2/9f
pu		ELIXIR DE NUTZ (FR)	10	11-10	(s+t)	Joe Tizzard	Freddie Gingell	40/1

6 ran Race Time 4m 12.00 Closing Sectional (3.75f): 61.0s (97.4%) Winning Owner: Declan Landy

The withdrawal of Jonbon due to the poor form of a lot of his stable's runners on the first day of the meeting seemingly deprived the race of the only threat to his old rival El Fabiolo, but the fences got in the way as he joined Douvan as a 9/2-on beaten favourite in this and, in a well-run race, others fell by the wayside as well, leaving the finish to be contested by a pair that had been well behind the favourite in the Dublin Chase last time out, the form average at best in a race that has had more than its share of renewals that failed to deliver in the last few years; the pace was good, the pace-setting Edwardstone on the retreat when he departed 2 out and likely to have run a below-par third. **Captain Guinness** finally won a Grade 1 after making the frame 8 times in such races, inferior to the likes of Energumene, El Fabiolo and Jonbon but able to take advantage of their absence/failure to complete on this occasion, not having to better the pick of his form to do so against a rival with a similar profile; in touch, travelled well, went second 4 out, led straight, looked in control last, idled run-in, edged right, ridden out. **Gentleman de Mee** who sweated up beforehand, ran well under a change of tactics, contesting his seventh successive Grade 1 chase, deserving credit for consistency since his Dublin Chase win last season, though as his record suggests he's vulnerable against the very best in the division; in rear, travelled well, ridden after 3 out, left second 2 out, kept on run-in. **Funambule Sivola** looks a shadow of the horse he was, but he's picked up 80 grand for turning up and getting around on his last 2 starts, so all credit to his connections for that; handy, raced freely, lost place ninth, tailed off 3 out. **Edwardstone** tried to repeat the tactics that had worked so well at Newbury, but he probably went a little faster than ideal and was on the retreat when he came down, likely to have run a fair way below his best; led, went with zest, shaken up after 3 out, headed straight, weakening when fell 2 out. **El Fabiolo** held outstanding claims, all the more so in the absence of Jonbon, but he fluffed his lines for the first time over fences; in touch, not fluent first, bad mistake fifth, pulled up. **Elixir de Nutz** wasn't in anything like the same form as last time, perhaps finding the ground softer than ideal; pressed leader early, tracked pace after, pushed along 4 out, dropped away soon after, pulled up straight.

Weatherbys Champion Bumper (Standard Open National Hunt Flat) (Grade 1) (1)

Pos	*Btn*	*Horse*	*Age*	*Wgt*	*Eq*	*Trainer*	*Jockey*	*SP*
1		JASMIN DE VAUX (FR)	5	11-7		W. P. Mullins, Ireland	Mr P. W. Mullins	9/2
2	1¾	ROMEO COOLIO	5	11-7		Gordon Elliott, Ireland	Keith Donoghue	18/1
3	2½	JALON D'OUDAIRIES (FR)	5	11-7		Gordon Elliott, Ireland	J. W. Kennedy	3/1f
4	1¼	SOUNDS VICTORIUS (IRE)	5	11-7		W. P. Mullins, Ireland	S. F. O'Keeffe	66/1
5	½	FISHERY LANE (FR)	5	11-7		W. P. Mullins, Ireland	M. J. M. O'Sullivan	66/1
6	6	THE YELLOW CLAY (IRE)	5	11-7		Gordon Elliott, Ireland	Jordan Colin Gainford	17/2
7	hd	FLEUR AU FUSIL (FR)	6	11-0	(h)	W. P. Mullins, Ireland	Miss Josephine Townend	10/1
8	5	ROYAL INFANTRY (IRE)	5	11-7		Dan Skelton	Harry Skelton	18/1
9	1½	UNION AVENUE (IRE)	5	11-7		James Moffatt	Danny McMenamin	125/1
10	2½	YOU OUGHTA KNOW (IRE)	6	11-7	(h)	W. P. Mullins, Ireland	D. E. Mullins	15/2
11	1¾	DIRTY DEN	4	10-11	(h)	Syd Hosie	Micheal Nolan	150/1
12	hd	TEESHAN (IRE)	5	11-7		Paul Nicholls	Harry Cobden	16/1
13	3½	C'EST TA CHANCE (FR)	5	11-7		W. P. Mullins, Ireland	Daryl Jacob	33/1
14	5½	ARGENTO BOY (IRE)	5	11-7		W. P. Mullins, Ireland	B. Hayes	18/1
15	11	BILL JOYCE (IRE)	5	11-7		Jonjo O'Neill	Jonjo O'Neill Jr.	7/1

16	hd	QUEBECOIS (FR)	5	11-7	Paul Nicholls	Lorcan Williams	66/1
17	¾	SIXMILEBRIDGE (IRE)	5	11-7	Ben Pauling	Kielan Woods	33/1
18	33	CANTICO (IRE)	5	11-7	W. P. Mullins, Ireland	P. Townend	11/1
pu		STAVVY (IRE)	4	10-11	Jane Chapple-Hyam	Bryony Frost	100/1

19 ran Race Time 4m 07.90 Closing Sectional (4.10f): 60.1s (103.1%) Winning Owner: Mr Simon Munir/Mr Isaac Souede

It was fitting that in landing the Champion Bumper Willie Mullins became the first trainer to send out a hundred winners at the Cheltenham Festival, this the race that he dominated even before he became all-powerful in other divisions, Jasmin de Vaux his thirteenth victory in the event and his fourth in the last 5 seasons; there were 5 withdrawals due to ground and other reasons, 4 from Britain and one from Mullins' yard, which left a field of 19, 8 trained in Britain, 8 by Mullins and the other 3 by Gordon Elliott, the last-named's trio helping the Irish take the first 7 places, British ones not at the races, the last home success, Ballyandy in 2016, becoming a distant memory; the race was soundly run, the first 2 smooth travellers that came from off the pace, one on each wing of the field down the hill, the principals a bit too closely bunched at the finish to take an especially high view of the form, though as ever this is a race that is set to throw up plenty of winners over jumps next season and beyond. **Jasmin de Vaux** down in trip, was much improved from debut, though he's more stayer than speedster and is likely a Baring Bingham/Spa candidate for next season rather than Supreme, one of the less taking of the Mullins team, needing to fill out still; raced wide, held up, travelled well, headway entering straight, stayed on to lead well inside final 1f, edged right, kept on well. **Romeo Coolio** was much improved from debut, plenty to like about the way he went through the race, sure to have a bright future over hurdles; raced along inside, held up, travelled well, smooth headway over 3f out, challenged entering straight, led over 1f out, headed well inside final 1f. **Jalon d'Oudairies** lost his unbeaten record but shaped with plenty of promise again, ridden much more prominently than the pair that beat him, having the physique to think he'll do well over hurdles and then fences in seasons to come; never far away, travelled well, led entering straight, headed over 1f out, one paced. **Sounds Victorius** up in grade, ran his best race, again looking a staying type, lacking the pace to land a blow in the straight; handy, shaken up 3f out, driven early in straight, kept on gradually. **Fishery Lane** one of 2 maidens in the field, was much improved from debut and might have done even better had he made his move earlier, all in all a promising effort from one that should make an impact over hurdles next season; held up, travelled well, shaken up home turn, ran green, edged left, kept on well final 1f, nearest at the finish. **The Yellow Clay** was strong in the betting, with decent form claims, though he was one of the more exposed runners and ran just respectably, probably keener than ideal; prominent, not settle fully, every chance home turn, wandered, no extra inside final 1f. **Fleur Au Fusil** the one mare in the field and one of only two 6-y-os that took their chance, ran creditably in first-time hood, though without quite being able to land a blow; held up, travelled well, effort 3f out, not quicken entering straight, no extra final 1f. **Royal Infantry** emerged best of the British, the third time since 2020 that his yard has supplied the best of the home team, his record and style of running suggesting one that will do well over hurdles beyond 2m next season; held up, steady headway approaching straight, ridden, one paced. **Union Avenue** who sweated up and was on his toes beforehand, ended up running surprisingly well, given that and the way he went through the race, not at all a bad type and with potential as a hurdler next season; waited with, went with little fluency, lost place end of back straight, plugged on, never on terms. **You Oughta Know** was well below his previous form in first-time hood, not seeing the race out; waited with, lost place end of back straight, effort 3f out, chased leaders briefly early in straight, weakened over 1f out. **Dirty Den** was flying too high in this grade; held up, shaken up 4f out, plugged on straight, never on terms. **Teeshan** ran below his debut form, his exertions in front telling in the latter stages; led, raced freely, shaken up 3f out, headed entering straight, weakened. **C'est Ta Chance** one of 2 maidens in the field, ran well below his debut form, likely that this was just too much for him at this early stage in his career; handy, shaken up over 3f out, dropped away early in straight. **Argento Boy** went backwards from his debut, looking still in need of experience once he came off the bridle; patiently ridden, headway end of back straight, every chance 3f out, shaken up, ran green, lost place soon after; he looks the part for jumping and should have a future, despite this reverse. **Bill Joyce** came into this unbeaten but found a much more competitive race all too much; in touch, bumped and lost place 4f out, labouring soon after. **Quebecois** had looked a useful prospect when winning at Exeter but was well held after 3 months off, one of the first in trouble, perhaps all not well with him; tracked pace, shaken up 4f out, weakened quickly. **Sixmilebridge** was well held, very weak in the betting and losing his race before the start, geed up and sweating throughout the preliminaries (the red hood no help and removed before he entered the paddock); prominent, not settle fully, shaken up over 4f out, lost place soon after. **Cantico** about the pick of the field on looks, shaped as if amiss; prominent, took keen hold, every chance 3f out, shaken up, weakened quickly, eased; he's best judged on previous efforts. **Stavvy** was out of his depth, though possibly had some problem given he failed to finish; chased leaders, labouring end of back straight, tailed off when pulled up 5f out.

CHELTENHAM Thursday March 14
SOFT

Turners Novices' Chase (Golden Miller) (Grade 1) (1)

Pos	Btn	Horse	Age	Wgt	Eq	Trainer	Jockey	SP
1		GREY DAWNING (IRE)	7	11-7		Dan Skelton	Harry Skelton	5/2jf
2	2	GINNY'S DESTINY (IRE)	8	11-7		Paul Nicholls	Harry Cobden	11/2
3	8	DJELO (FR)	6	11-7		Venetia Williams	Charlie Deutsch	25/1
4	2½	ZANAHIYR (IRE)	7	11-7	(s+t)	Gordon Elliott, Ireland	J. W. Kennedy	17/2
5	1¾	IROKO (FR)	6	11-7	(t)	Oliver Greenall & Josh Guerriero	Jonjo O'Neill Jr.	13/2
6	3	COLONEL HARRY (IRE)	7	11-7	(t)	Jamie Snowden	Gavin Sheehan	28/1
7	hd	FACILE VEGA (IRE)	7	11-7		W. P. Mullins, Ireland	P. Townend	5/2jf
8	6½	LETSBECLEARABOUTIT (IRE)	9	11-7		Gavin Patrick Cromwell, Ireland	Keith Donoghue	12/1
9	31	SHARJAH (FR)	11	11-7	(t)	W. P. Mullins, Ireland	Mr P. W. Mullins	25/1
pu		JAMAICO (FR)	5	11-5	(t)	David Pipe	Jack Tudor	150/1
pu		LE PATRON (FR)	6	11-7		Gary Moore	David Noonan	100/1

11 ran Race Time 5m 05.40 Closing Sectional (3.84f): 59.40s (99.9%) Winning Owner: Mr Robert Kirkland

A tremendous spectacle and not just for followers of British jump racing who'd had to live on a diet of handicaps over the first couple of days, the 2 big home-trained hopes going hammer and tongs from 3 out, the 2 of them and Djelo already having opened up a gap on the rest by that point, both calling on all the qualities that had seen them chisel themselves to the top of the domestic pecking order among the novice chasers to push their ratings a bit higher still, the timefigure underpinning the form. **Grey Dawning** had been given more of a break having been kept quite busy through the depths of the winter and, running here in preference to taking on Fact To File in the Broadway, proved his trainer bang on the money for the umpteenth time this week, Grey Dawning cementing his status as the leading British-trained novice, seemingly having learnt no end from the mistake that cost him victory over Ginny's Destiny here in December; jumping superbly tracking the pace, he jumped on 2 out when his old rival got in a bit tight and, having looked in control at the last, edged right on the run-in to leave the door ajar briefly before asserting in the final 100 yds; he could well go to Aintree, while a clash with the aforementioned Fact To File and others is something to look forward to next season with even more improvement on the cards (remains unexposed as a stayer). **Ginny's Destiny** has also upped his game appreciably since rather fortuitiously beating Grey Dawning here in December, having to give best to his old rival on 3 lb worse terms but confirming himself the second best novice chaser in Britain with another polished display; led, jumped soundly in main and travelled fluently, tackled 3 out, headed when getting in a bit close to the next, rallied run-in as the winner edged right, no extra only near the finish; given how well he goes at this course a return for the Paddy Power in the autumn will presumably be the aim, and there's probably even better to come, this his first season with Nicholls. **Djelo** sweating beforehand, ran as well as could be expected, handy until a bit outpaced by the first pair 3 out, plugging on in their wake in the straight; he's younger than the first 2 and another for whom the Paddy Power would look a likely target in the autumn. **Zanahiyr** who attracted some support, matched his form in maiden chases, doing best of the Irish, but is yet to get within 10 lb of his best hurdles form in this sphere; settled in touch, untidy 3 out, stayed on from next without threatening to get near the leaders. **Iroko** had initially been ruled out for the season after impressing at Warwick in the autumn and, although he recovered from a foot injury in time to take his chance, he looked rusty as well as inexperienced, unable to play much of a part; mid-field, lost ground approaching 4 out, not fluent there, no threat after and pecked next, plugged on latter stages; this experience should really benefit him and he remains open to improvement, particularly back over 3m+. **Colonel Harry** was never involved from out the back but did at least run on past a few late, and he's unexposed at this trip at a realistic level on very testing ground. **Facile Vega** sweating and unimpressive in condition, hasn't taken to chasing as well as expected and was found wanting in the jumping department here, failing to convince with his stamina for this longer trip either, acknowleging that jumping and having to make up ground in a race that didn't favour such tactics might have had a bearing on that; held up, untidy at the third, fifth and most notably the tenth, crept closer 4 out but faltered from 2 out; it wouldn't be a huge surprise to see him back over hurdles at Punchestown. **Letsbeclearaboutit** was backed at long odds but couldn't get competitive, whether he was in the right race a moot point given how he performed; raced off the pace, not fluent second, some headway before 3 out, effort proved short-lived. **Sharjah** placed at 3 Festivals over hurdles, including in 2 Champion Hurdles, has some smart form over fences but ran no sort of race this time; dropped out, hampered first, made no impression whatsoever. **Jamaico** was out of his depth on first outing since leaving Emmanuel Clayeux after 9 months off; chased leaders, mistakes fifth, ninth, lost place next. **Le Patron** ran even worse, already starting to struggle when clouting the tenth.

Ryanair Chase (Festival Trophy) (Grade 1) (1)

Pos	Btn	Horse	Age	Wgt	Eq	Trainer	Jockey	SP
1		PROTEKTORAT (FR)	9	11-10	(t)	Dan Skelton	Harry Skelton	17/2
2	4	ENVOI ALLEN (FR)	10	11-10	(t)	Henry de Bromhead, Ireland	Rachael Blackmore	9/4f
3	2¾	CONFLATED (IRE)	10	11-10		Gordon Elliott, Ireland	J. W. Kennedy	11/1
4	nk	CAPODANNO (FR)	8	11-10	(t)	W. P. Mullins, Ireland	M. P. Walsh	9/1
5	4½	STAGE STAR (IRE)	8	11-10		Paul Nicholls	Harry Cobden	6/1
6	6½	AHOY SENOR (IRE)	9	11-10		Lucinda Russell	Derek Fox	18/1
7	1¾	FIL DOR (FR)	6	11-10	(t)	Gordon Elliott, Ireland	Keith Donoghue	28/1
8	15	HITMAN (FR)	8	11-10	(s+t)	Paul Nicholls	Bryony Frost	40/1
9	40	BANBRIDGE (IRE)	8	11-10		Joseph Patrick O'Brien, Ireland	J. J. Slevin	4/1
pu		FUGITIF (FR)	9	11-10	(s+t)	Richard Hobson	Sean Bowen	16/1
pu		GA LAW (FR)	8	11-10	(s)	Jamie Snowden	Gavin Sheehan	22/1

11 ran Race Time 5m 21.60 Closing Sectional (3.84f): 58s (103.5%) Winning Owner: Sir A Ferguson G Mason J Hales & L Hales

A second year in a row lacking an imperious Mullins-trained contender, which did probably encourage a couple of new faces to try their hand here instead of in something else on the week, one from that group proving too strong late on for a defending champion who ran to something like his best again. **Protektorat** added a Ryanair Chase to his prior Grade 1 success in the Betfair, campaigned as a stayer since then but no sluggard and appearing to find this intermediate trip in the mud a sweetspot, having no trouble tracking a brisk pace and, moved up to press Stage Star entering the straight, producing a more fluent leap than the challenging favourite to move on at the last before seeing things out thoroughly to draw clear; it likely won't last till the close of play on Friday but Skelton getting to this point only a couple of winners behind the all-conquering Willie Mullins—with Nicholls and Henderson boasting just 1 between them—ranks as one of the most notable training performances by a British yard at the meeting in recent years. **Envoi Allen** had to settle for second in his bid to defend his crown, even back in trip proving vulnerable to a stronger stayer 4 months on from Down Royal, a mistake at the last when upsides the winner impacting the distance beaten but not the result for all he'd swept alongside on the bridle in the straight under a patient ride; it will likely get lost among the narrative of Mullins hegemony but his yard has delivered at the meeting yet again, certainly so in the non-handicaps with 2 winners over the first 3 days joined by a further 6 frame finishers from just 10 runners in the graded races. **Conflated** was ridden differently to usual in the wrong circumstances dropping back from 3m for the first time in a while, likely to have gone close had more use been made of him, as it was the similarly-campaigned winner; held up, effort entering straight, not quicken 2 out, rallied well flat, finished with running left. **Capodanno** upheld and more Cotswold dominance over Ahoy Senor but still left the impression dropping back in distance didn't bring his proven stamina sufficiently into play, especially ridden as he was, keeping mistakes to a minimum for a change after ballooning the first but staying on rather than quickening as required having switched inside for his move before 2 out. **Stage Star** did about all he could trying to pull off the same tactics that have served him so well around here, forced into going rather harder than in either the Turners or Paddy Power but not lying down once tackled by the first 2, holding on to his lead until before the last and tying up only late on. **Ahoy Senor** continued his season's blank, a trademark error coming at the worst time kept to a trip short of his best; pressed leader, upsides briefly eighth, clouted 3 out, rallied until straight, left behind gradually. **Fil Dor** fell some way short beyond Grade 3 level in open company for the umpteenth time after 3 months off, shaving only a fraction (£2561.63) off the vast sum his new owners had paid to get hold of him out of the Caldwell dispersal; dropped out, pushed along approaching straight, made little impression. **Hitman** wasn't in the same form as last time above all, not going for nearly as long on the bridle for one; settled in touch, lost place out wide home turn, faltered 2 out. **Banbridge** will be well worth another chance to give his yard another Melling Chase when going for back-to-back Aintree successes next month, assuming of course the ground comes in his favour again, allowed to take his chance here 9 weeks on from his sprightly reappearance only to underline his reliance these days on less testing conditions; tracked pace, lost place when slow 4 out, soon done with next. **Fugitif** turned in a rare poor Cheltenham effort up in grade, not showing the zip to derive any benefit from the return to a more suitable trip; soon behind, never going pace, struggling when clouted eleventh. **Ga Law** was let down by his jumping back up in grade; raced off the pace, hit eighth, 5 out, no chance after.

Paddy Power Stayers' Hurdle (Grade 1) (1)

Pos	*Btn*	*Horse*	*Age*	*Wgt*	*Eq*	*Trainer*	*Jockey*	*SP*
1		TEAHUPOO (FR)	7	11-10		Gordon Elliott, Ireland	J. W. Kennedy	5/4f
2	3¾	FLOORING PORTER (IRE)	9	11-10	(t)	Gavin Patrick Cromwell, Ireland	Keith Donoghue	9/1
3	2¼	HOME BY THE LEE (IRE)	9	11-10	(b)	Joseph Patrick O'Brien, Ireland	J. J. Slevin	16/1
4	2¼	BUDDY ONE (IRE)	7	11-10		Paul John Gilligan, Ireland	Jack G. Gilligan	40/1
5	2½	SIRE DU BERLAIS (FR)	12	11-10	(b+t)	Gordon Elliott, Ireland	M. P. Walsh	14/1
6	1	ASTERION FORLONGE (FR)	10	11-10	(t)	W. P. Mullins, Ireland	Mr P. W. Mullins	33/1
7	½	NOBLE YEATS (IRE)	9	11-10	(s+t)	Emmet Mullins, Ireland	Harry Cobden	7/1
8	hd	DASHEL DRASHER	11	11-10		Jeremy Scott	Rex Dingle	16/1
9	2	CRAMBO	7	11-10	(t)	Fergal O'Brien	Jonathan Burke	7/1
10	nk	PAISLEY PARK (IRE)	12	11-10	(t)	Emma Lavelle	Tom Bellamy	14/1
11	15	JANIDIL (FR)	10	11-10	(s+t)	W. P. Mullins, Ireland	Jody McGarvey	66/1
12	11	SIR GERHARD (IRE)	9	11-10		W. P. Mullins, Ireland	P. Townend	9/1

12 ran Race Time 6m 08.80 Closing Sectional (3.80f): 54.9s (106.5%) Winning Owner: Robcour

A relatively recent addition to the staying hurdle scene in a race full of veterans made up for his misfortune on his first crack at the race in 2023, though another stop-start gallop and resulting bunched finish in behind—plus the proximity of a couple of apparent no-hopers who helped make up a 1-2-3-4-5-6-7 for the Irish contingent as the British challenge sunk without trace—merely underlined the position that the division is open at the minute but far from stellar in terms of standard, merely running to his reappearance form enough to see Teahupoo set himself apart late on from a dual previous all-the-way winner who wasn't moved to the front this time until after the fourth. **Teahupoo** capitalised on the Champion Hurdle rerouting of the same connections' Irish Point as he confirmed impressions from the Hatton's Grace, crucially kept fresh since (now 5-5 when returning from at least 3 months off) and, heavily backed with conditions having come right as well, forging his way to the lead running to the last and sustaining his run to go clear on the flat, a minor error 2 out as he closed in out wide and a move back inside on the home turn that tightened up Noble Yeats not enough trouble to see a repeat of his less-than-charmed passage in 2023; he's still got youth on his side when so many in the division are at or nearing the end of their career, though so too does Irish Point, which may well signal the start of an Elliott stranglehold at the top of the staying hurdling tree. **Flooring Porter** found an up-and-comer 2 years his junior too good but did all he could under a less gung-ho ride than in 2023, taking his record in the race to 1142 with chasing sensibly shelved following his last couple of runs the other side of the New Year; he didn't adopt his usual front-running position until before the fifth this time and hardly took off even once there, but he'd pressed on by the home turn and just couldn't shake off Teahupoo, already headed and put in his place when crossed and forced to switch approaching the last. **Home By The Lee** returned to his best on his first run since Christmas, a change of headgear (first-time blinkers) adding a spark and the aborting of the front-running role clearly in his favour, claiming the placing this year that a bad mistake had perhaps denied him on his second crack at this in 2023; held up, headway 2 out, not quicken early in straight, wandered before last, rallied. **Buddy One** surpassed expectations as he left behind his first 2 runs at this level returning from 11 weeks off, putting a cap on a season of progress that began with defeats in handicaps from ITC marks in the mid-high 130s; in touch, effort on inner straight, kept on. **Sire du Berlais** couldn't add to one of the best Cheltenham Festival records of recent times but had shown there's still plenty left by the end in a race that didn't develop in quite the same advantageous way as the 2023 running, flat out from the eighth and still labouring in last entering the straight only to pass more than half the field from there, finishing with a flourish; still fresh after his delayed comeback, another attempt to defend a Grade 1 crown beckons at Aintree next month. **Asterion Forlonge** ran about as well as could be expected after 11 weeks off, his limitations long since exposed; pressed leader, jumped more fluently than usual, led second, headed before fifth, blundered eighth, outpaced home turn. **Noble Yeats** confirmed Cleeve superiority over a couple with cheekpieces back on but was still some way short of adding another notable chapter to his storied career; led until second, tracked pace after, ridden when snatched up entering straight, left behind gradually; this should put him spot on for the Grand National, for which he'll have frame claims again from a mark 1 lb lower than when fourth in 2023. **Dashel Drasher** did best of the British for the second year in a row but was clearly some way below those 2023 heights in a race that in general gave a sizeable knock to the form of the earlier major graded staying prizes on these shores; tracked pace, lost place when not fluent sixth, driven after 2 out, not quicken. **Crambo** failed to make the required extra step forward as he trailed in some way behind a fellow 7-y-o who did perform, saving him for this since Ascot before Christmas possibly backfiring given how he'd been thriving on his racing back then; held up, outpaced before 2 out, made little impression. **Paisley Park** brought the curtain down on a memorable career, one highlighted by his stirring win in the 2019 renewal on his first of a remarkable 6 runs in the race; British jumps racing won't seem quite the same without him. **Janidil** made little appeal on recent chasing form and, unproven at the trip as well, didn't get home tried in cheekpieces after 9 weeks off; dropped out, mistake third, some headway home turn, weakened. **Sir Gerhard** doesn't really have a suitable race at this meeting, 3m not unsurprisingly beyond him after he'd taken a strong hold held up out wide, though he also looked awkward (hung left) when making the brief move that he did.

Ryanair Mares' Novices' Hurdle (Dawn Run) (Grade 2) (1)

Pos	*Btn*	*Horse*	*Age*	*Wgt*	*Eq*	*Trainer*	*Jockey*	*SP*
1		GOLDEN ACE	6	11-2		Jeremy Scott	Lorcan Williams	10/1
2	1¾	BRIGHTERDAYSAHEAD (FR)	5	11-7		Gordon Elliott, Ireland	J. W. Kennedy	5/6f
3	1¾	BIRDIE OR BUST (IRE)	6	11-7		Henry de Bromhead, Ireland	Rachael Blackmore	10/1
4	½	JADE DE GRUGY (FR)	5	11-7		W. P. Mullins, Ireland	P. Townend	2/1
5	10	MAJESTIC FORCE (IRE)	6	11-2		Henry de Bromhead, Ireland	D. J. O'Keeffe	25/1

6	3¼	MOLLYS MANGO	6	11-2	(t)	Harry Derham	Paul O'Brien	40/1
7	2¾	TITANIUM MOON	6	11-2		Donald McCain	Brian Hughes	80/1
8	4	VICTORIA MILANO (IRE)	6	11-2		Alastair Ralph	Jack Tudor	125/1

8 ran Race Time 4m 20.80 Closing Sectional (3.80f): 53.0s (111.2%) Winning Owner: Mr I. F. Gosden

Probably no greater example of the doom and gloom surrounding British jump racing from Tuesday and Wednesday receding on Day 3 than this result, Golden Ace—British bred to boot—striking a blow for the smaller yard in downing a few unbeaten Irish mares and becoming the third British-trained winner in succession of a race whose first 6 runnings had gone across the Irish Sea; the rest of the field rather left the outsider alone in front and the result was a still congested field 2 out and a relative sprint for home, which suited the winner far better than the runner-up. **Golden Ace** was left as the leading home-trained hope when Dysart Enos—who'd walloped her to the tune of 9 lengths in last year's mares' bumper at Aintree—was withdrawn through lameness on the morning of the race, and maintained her unbeaten record over hurdles in downing a posse of Irish-trained mares, from 3 of whom she received 5 lb, the slow gallop and relative emphasis on speed suiting her much more than the runner-up in particular; waited with out wide travelling strongly, she made headway going well 2 out and, after edging ahead well before the last, quickened a little way clear late on; for all she had things in her favour here, she can do better still, and would be a fascinating runner against the boys at Aintree, though Punchestown will presumably come under consideration too. **Brighterdaysahead** very much a chaser in appearance and sporting a red hood in the preliminaries, might have lost her unbeaten record but still put up the best performance in the race—like the next couple home she gave the winner 5 lb—despite the slow pace seeming all against her, not settling fully and still taking a bit of a grip levelling for home; in touch, untidy fifth, upsides briefly early in straight, stayed on but lacked speed of winner; she's got time on her side as a 5-y-o and remains capable of better, particularly back in a more well-run race and/or back up in trip. **Birdie Or Bust** after 12 weeks off and on her toes beforehand, ran her best race, well positioned on the one hand the way this developed but again looking a horse that will benefit from going up in trip, and she's open to further improvement with that in mind; chased leader before second, led when not fluent 2 out, headed before last, jumped left there, edged right run-in, kept on. **Jade de Grugy** lost her unbeaten record but left the distinct impression that this didn't get near the bottom of her; tracked pace, took strong hold, short of room on landing 2 out and shuffled back a bit, effort on inner straight, one paced; definitely remains capable of better. **Majestic Force** coming here on the back of one point and one small-field maiden hurdle over 2½m (successful in both), and that lack of experience, together with the way this developed, seemed to count against her; patiently ridden, short of room approaching home turn, plugged on, never landed a blow; remains capable of better. **Mollys Mango** picked up for €170,000 at the Caldwell Construction dispersal sale (formerly trained by Gordon Elliott), was a touch disappointing in a first-time tongue strap after 10 weeks off, though she hasn't been long with her new yard and it's probably best not to judge her on this slowly-run contest; in rear, going well when in touch out wide 2 out, not quicken straight. **Titanium Moon** faced a stiff task in this grade, while the slow gallop seemed against her, too; held up, not settle fully, not fluent 2 out, short of room soon after, outpaced straight. **Victoria Milano** was out of her depth; dictated, not fluent fourth, slow 3 out, headed when not fluent next, brushed aside.

CHELTENHAM Friday March 15

HEAVY

JCB Triumph Hurdle (Grade 1) (1)

Pos	Btn	Horse	Age	Wgt	Eq	Trainer	Jockey	SP
1		MAJBOROUGH (FR)	4	11-2		W. P. Mullins, Ireland	M. P. Walsh	6/1
2	1½	KARGESE (FR)	4	10-9	(h)	W. P. Mullins, Ireland	D. E. Mullins	4/1
3	4¾	SALVER (FR)	4	11-2		Gary Moore	Gavin Sheehan	10/1
4	7½	NURBURGRING (IRE)	4	11-2	(t)	Joseph Patrick O'Brien, Ireland	J. J. Slevin	6/1
5	1	STORM HEART (FR)	4	11-2		W. P. Mullins, Ireland	P. Townend	7/2f
6	2¼	SALVATOR MUNDI (FR)	4	11-2	(h+t)	W. P. Mullins, Ireland	B. Hayes	17/2
7	3¾	BUNTING (FR)	4	11-2		W. P. Mullins, Ireland	S. F. O'Keeffe	11/2
8	19	ITHACA'S ARROW	4	11-2		Dominic Ffrench Davis	Ben Ffrench Davis	150/1
9	½	HIGHWIND (FR)	4	11-2		W. P. Mullins, Ireland	Rachael Blackmore	33/1
10	11	ETHICAL DIAMOND (IRE)	4	11-2		W. P. Mullins, Ireland	M. J. M. O'Sullivan	25/1
pu		FRATAS (IRE)	4	10-9		Michael Mulvany, Ireland	D. J. O'Keeffe	66/1
pu		MIGHTY BANDIT (IRE)	4	11-2		Warren Greatrex	James Bowen	28/1

12 ran Race Time 4m 18.70 Closing Sectional (3.80f): 57.4s (101.9%) Winning Owner: Mr John P. McManus

The travails of the Nicky Henderson yard had deprived the Festival of quite a few high-profile contenders, perhaps none more significant than Sir Gino, the short-priced favourite for the Triumph until the start of the week, the race having a much more open look for his absence, British stables left with just 3 representatives, notably the Finale winner Salver and the €420,000 purchase Mighty Bandit, 4 of the main Irish contenders having taken the first 4 places in the Spring Juvenile Hurdle—all 4 trained by Willie Mullins—Nurburgring and the once-raced Salvator Mundi, in the same ownership as Sir Gino, also plausible candidates; the race was run at a steady pace, under testing conditions, developing only 2 out, the first 2 doing well to pull clear, the imposing winner turning the tables on the second from the Spring, his performance well up to standard for the race, suggesting Sir Gino wouldn't have had things all his own way had he been able to take his chance. **Majborough** an imposing type, the clear pick of the field on looks, had clearly learnt plenty from his run at Leopardstown, showing quite a bit of improvement to turn the tables on the runner-up, still looking pretty raw under pressure but knuckling down after the last; in touch, took keen hold, went prominent fifth, shaken up straight, every chance when jumped left last, led final 1f, ridden out; will go on improving, is sure to stay beyond 2m and in the longer term is an exciting prospect for novice chasing. **Kargese** went through the race much as she had in the Spring and looked the likely winner once she went to the front, but the winner had learnt from his last run against her and outstayed her late on, her effort nonetheless a good one, no surprise to see her aimed at the Mares' Hurdle in a year's time; led first, settled in touch but still very keen, smooth headway 2 out, led on bridle entering straight, shaken up before last, headed final 1f, not quicken; the Anniversary Hurdle at Aintree should be perfect for her, though Sir Gino could be back by then, of course. **Salver** lost his unbeaten record over hurdles, having had something to find against the best of the Irish, but ran his best race all the same, albeit having been in a good position the way the race developed; close up, led before 3 out, headed entering straight, one paced. **Nurburgring** wasn't disgraced after 11 weeks off, poorly positioned when the tempo lifted, worth rating better than the result as a consequence; held up, effort 2 out, headway approaching last, kept on. **Storm Heart** strong in the betting, seemingly the stable first string and closely matched with the principals from the Spring, ran below form, having his chance in the straight but unable to finish the race so well as those in the frame, despite having looked a staying type last time; waited with, travelled well, headway when untidy fifth, challenged approaching last, weakened run-in; he lacks the scope of a few of the others. **Salvator Mundi** runner-up to Sir Gino in a listed newcomers hurdle at Auteuil last April for David Cottin, has a fair bit about him physically and, despite having got on his toes beforehand, shaped promisingly, facing such a stern task after an absence, sure to build on this with a run under his belt; held up, not fluent 3 out, headway early in straight, effort flattened out. **Bunting** closely matched with the principals from the Spring, looks the part for jumping, but he wasn't able to repeat that effort, perhaps wanting a more truly-run race; in touch, left behind 2 out. **Ithaca's Arrow** wasn't good enough to hold his position once the race developed fully, reported to be showing signs of post-race ataxia; prominent, mistake first, led briefly 3 out, shaken up home turn, weakened quickly. **Highwind** didn't have such a problem with jumping on this occasion but was still well below the form he'd shown last time; held up, not settle fully, left behind 2 out. **Ethical Diamond** had shaped encouragingly behind the principals when a big price last time but wasn't in the same form; waited with, left behind before 2 out. **Fratas** after 4 months off, failed to repeat her debut effort in this much tougher grade, not helping her cause by racing so keenly; led after first, headed before 3 out, weakened quickly, pulled up before last. **Mighty Bandit** bought for €420,000 from Gordon Elliott's yard since his flop at Christmas and given a breathing operation, was easy to back and shaped with limited encouragement, albeit highly tried; held up, not settle fully, shaken up before 2 out, left behind, pulled up last.

Albert Bartlett Novices' Hurdle (Spa) (Grade 1) (1)

Pos	*Btn*	*Horse*	*Age*	*Wgt*	*Eq*	*Trainer*	*Jockey*	*SP*
1		STELLAR STORY (IRE)	7	11-7	(s)	Gordon Elliott, Ireland	Sam Ewing	33/1
2	hd	THE JUKEBOX MAN (IRE)	6	11-7		Ben Pauling	Kielan Woods	18/1
3	7	DANCING CITY (FR)	7	11-7		W. P. Mullins, Ireland	D. E. Mullins	8/1
4	¾	SPREAD BOSS TED	7	11-7		W. P. Mullins, Ireland	S. F. O'Keeffe	40/1
5	sh	LECKY WATSON (IRE)	6	11-7	(h)	W. P. Mullins, Ireland	B. Hayes	16/1
6	8	GIDLEIGH PARK	6	11-7		Harry Fry	Jonathan Burke	9/2
7	1¾	SEARCH FOR GLORY (IRE)	7	11-7	(b+t)	Gordon Elliott, Ireland	J. W. Kennedy	22/1
8	7½	JOHNNYWHO (IRE)	7	11-7	(t)	Jonjo O'Neill	Jonjo O'Neill Jr.	16/1
9	5	DRIPSEY MOON (IRE)	7	11-7		John McConnell, Ireland	B. W. Harvey	200/1
10	24	CAPTAIN TEAGUE (IRE)	6	11-7		Paul Nicholls	Harry Cobden	6/1
11	3	CHIGORIN (IRE)	6	11-7		Henry de Bromhead, Ireland	Rachael Blackmore	12/1
pu		HIGH CLASS HERO	7	11-7		W. P. Mullins, Ireland	Mr P. W. Mullins	10/1
pu		READIN TOMMY WRONG (IRE)	6	11-7		W. P. Mullins, Ireland	P. Townend	2/1f

13 ran Race Time 6m 24.50 Closing Sectional (3.80f): 57.9s (105.3%) Winning Owner: Gigginstown House Stud

A representative field for the Spa, if a smaller one than usual, and the most open-looking of the novice hurdles during the week, though it proved a little unsatisfactory, the pace sedate for much of the way, the first 3 in those positions throughout, a few racing more keenly than ideal and then being in an unhelpful position when the tempo increased; that said, the race again went to a runner that improved significantly for the singular nature of the test, now 11 years since the race was won by the favourite, only one winner since sent off at single-figure odds, such prices no bar to them going on to show a high level of form, particularly over fences, the same likely to be true of this one—and runner-up, come to that—many in the field having the look of a chaser about them. **Stellar Story** showed much improved form, a race that drew out his stamina, despite the steady pace and a good position, very much playing to his strengths; tracked pace, not fluent 3 out, ridden after, every chance 2 out, not quicken early in straight, rallied well run-in, led dying strides; he's very much the type for chasing and seems sure to be a leading staying novice next season. **The Jukebox Man** was denied a surprise Grade 1 win in agonising fashion, very much having the run of the race and looking almost certain to win after kicking away from the field in the straight (touched 1.03 IR), only to be worn down by a stout stayer close home, this effort still his best, his physique, like so many here, suggesting a chaser for next season; led, jumped well, travelled well, kicked on after 2 out, clear last, tied up inside final 1f, caught dying strides. **Dancing City** well ahead of the winner last time, was unable to confirm the form, in a similar position but not staying on nearly so well; tracked pace, travelled well, shaken up entering straight, not quicken. **Spread Boss Ted** was stepping up markedly in grade and trip and did well, particularly as he was surely inconvenienced by his position, coming from the back of the field, the first 3 having been in those positions all the way; held up, effort 2 out, went fourth early in straight, one paced run-in. **Lecky Watson** fourth in the Champion Bumper last season, again ran with credit at the Festival, even though he was typically keen, despite a hood having been fitted, his demeanour very much that of a prospective chaser; held up, not settle fully, effort 2 out, not quicken approaching last. **Gidleigh Park** the pick on looks, lost his unbeaten record, his performance suggesting he'd have been better off in the Baring Bingham, even if he's bred to stay 3m; held up, not settle fully, effort after 3 out, made no impression; he's an exciting novice chase prospect for next winter. **Search For Glory** in a change of headgear, ran respectably taking on much tougher company, a winner twice at graded level but essentially a horse waiting for fences; in touch, hit 3 out, effort 2 out, not quicken straight. **Johnnywho** might have been expected to benefit from this increased test of stamina but was again below the form he showed in the Challow; in touch, chased leaders 2 out, weakened early in straight; he's been a shade disappointing on his last 2 starts, but he's been highly tried and on looks and pedigree he'll make a better chaser next season. **Dripsey Moon** faced a stiff task in this grade; held up, left behind 2 out. **Captain Teague** looked a leading contender for this after his win in the Challow (when he'd beaten the runner-up) but wasn't in the same form, not staying the extra distance nearly so well as might have been expected; waited with, travelled well, shaken up 2 out, weakened straight; he's a largely positive profile, and looks very much the type to make an impact in novice chases next season. **Chigorin** geed up beforehand and keener than ideal in the race, was well held after 3 months off, this experience too much for him at this early stage of his career; held up, not settle fully, not fluent first, left behind before 2 out. **High Class Hero** one of the less taking runners on looks, came into the race unbeaten, but this was much his stiffest task and he ran poorly, the longer trip neither here nor there; held up, mistake eighth, left behind before 2 out, pulled up straight. **Readin Tommy Wrong** strong in the betting and his stable's first string, looked to have plenty going for him, but he flopped, a rare reverse for his yard this week, one of several in the race that were too keen due to the steady pace; waited with, took strong hold, lost place before 2 out, pulled up last; he has the size for fences.

Boodles Cheltenham Gold Cup Chase (Grade 1) (1)

Pos	Btn	Horse	Age	Wgt	Eq	Trainer	Jockey	SP
1		GALOPIN DES CHAMPS (FR)	8	11-10		W. P. Mullins, Ireland	P. Townend	10/11f
2	3½	GERRI COLOMBE (FR)	8	11-10		Gordon Elliott, Ireland	J. W. Kennedy	13/2
3	9½	CORACH RAMBLER (IRE)	10	11-10	(t)	Lucinda Russell	Derek Fox	14/1

4	2¼	L'HOMME PRESSE (FR)	9	11-10		Venetia Williams	Charlie Deutsch	16/1
5	3½	BRAVEMANSGAME (FR)	9	11-10		Paul Nicholls	Harry Cobden	14/1
6	1¾	JUNGLE BOOGIE (IRE)	10	11-10		Henry de Bromhead, Ireland	Rachael Blackmore	16/1
ur		FASTORSLOW (FR)	8	11-10	(t)	Martin Brassil, Ireland	J. J. Slevin	8/1
pu		GENTLEMANSGAME	8	11-10		M. F. Morris, Ireland	D. J. O'Keeffe	25/1
pu		MONKFISH (IRE)	10	11-10		W. P. Mullins, Ireland	Mr P. W. Mullins	18/1
pu		NASSALAM (FR)	7	11-10	(b)	Gary Moore	Niall Houlihan	33/1
pu		THE REAL WHACKER (IRE)	8	11-10	(v)	Patrick Neville	Sam Twiston-Davies	40/1

11 ran Race Time 7m 05.40 Closing Sectional (3.84f): 62.80s (98.8%) Winning Owner: Mrs Audrey Turley

The centennial running of the Cheltenham Gold Cup, initially in the shadow of the National Hunt Chase at this meeting, as well as the Grand National, but firmly established in the modern era as the blue riband of steeplechasing, a superb test of stamina and jumping, the former to the fore in this running, the time taken over 7 minutes for just the third time this century—the runnings won by Bobs Worth and Native River, both thorough stayers, the others; the field was dominated by last season's winner Galopin des Champs, who had won both of the 3m Grade 1s run at Leopardstown this winter, the next 2 in the market horses he'd beaten in those, the home defence headed by last season's runner-up, a Grand National winner and the 2022 Broadway victor, the King George winner Hewick, due to the ground, and Shishkin, due to stable form, both notable absentees; the race was soundly run, plenty of competition for the lead over the first 2 fences, before the shape of the race became clear, the 6 finishers all still in contention 3 out, though the winner was going ominously well and stamped his authority on the race in the straight, not needing to run quite to the level he did last season but confirming himself one of the better Gold Cup winners in recent times. **Galopin des Champs** who'd looked a superior Gold Cup winner in landing this race last season, had been beaten twice since, but he'd won both of the 3m Grade 1s run at Leopardstown this winter and stood out on form, even in a good field, the defence of his crown always going smoothly, finding plenty too under much more testing conditions than in 2023; tracked pace, jumped soundly, travelled well, shaken up entering straight, led 2 out, in command soon after, ridden run-in, kept on well; there are some good novices among the current crop, but he'll be very much the one to beat in this next season, if all goes well, holding a great chance to be the first 3-time winner of the Cheltenham Gold Cup since Best Mate. **Gerri Colombe** proved much more competitive against the winner than he had at Christmas, given a break since, and ran the race of his life, looking well suited by the extra emphasis on stamina, minor jumping errors in the latter stages not helping his cause, though he was beaten fair and square; never far away, not fluent 4 out, ridden after, every chance when mistake 2 out, not quicken, kept on well run-in, no impression on winner; he won at Aintree after finishing second at Cheltenham last season and could well follow that route again, with the Bowl the obvious option. **Corach Rambler** had plenty to find in this company and ran a cracker after 4 months off, looking as if he might do even better at the last (within 2 lengths of the runner-up) until his effort told late on, this still a superb Grand National trial, very much the one to beat as he bids for a second victory at Aintree even if his current odds make him less appealing from a betting point of view; dropped out, pushed along early final circuit, ridden before 3 out, still plenty to do entering straight, good progress 2 out, went third last, tied up final 100 yds. **L'Homme Presse** looked in fine shape and acquitted himself well, better than the result, paying late on for his exertions against superior rivals; pressed leader, not fluent fifth, fourteenth, led briefly fifteenth, went on 4 out, shaken up straight, headed 2 out, weakened last; he disappointed as a novice at Aintree after winning the Broadway, though the ground was against him, that the key to his chance if he turns up in the Bowl. **Bravemansgame** as in 2022/23, had been off since the King George but he was unable to repeat his second placing to Galopin des Champs of last season, his form this winter generally a notch below where he was last; in touch, went prominent circuit out, shaken up 4 out, dropped away straight; he ran a fine race at Punchestown after this race last season, that the likeliest option for another appearance this spring. **Jungle Boogie** over 3f longer trip, looked to have plenty to find on just his fourth start over fences and seemed to excel himself upped in grade, plenty to like about the way he went through the race, a shame that he has stood so little racing; held up, still going well when mistake 3 out, ridden after, weakened approaching last. **Fastorslow** had twice got the better of Galopin des Champs since his defeat by Corach Rambler in the Ultima last season and had run well against him last time (breathing operation since), unfortunate that he didn't get the chance to show what he could do on this stage; tracked pace, yet to be asked for effort when unseated rider sixteenth. **Gentlemansgame** off 4 months since winning the Charlie Hall, wasn't in the same form, faced with his stiffest test to date; handy, not fluent eleventh, lost place circuit out, left behind 4 out, pulled up straight. **Monkfish** has 2 Cheltenham Festival wins to his name and had looked a contender for this race in his prime, but he's had very little racing in the last 3 years and couldn't build on his successful return over hurdles, faced with this much sterner task; held up, not fluent seventh, pushed along early final circuit, not fluent eighteenth, weakened next, pulled up before 2 out, bled. **Nassalam** looked outclassed in this field beforehand and found the company beyond him; raced off the pace, mistake second, pushed along early final circuit, hit seventeenth, tailed off after, pulled up; he's been clobbered by the handicapper for his Welsh National win (has to give 2 lb to Corach Rambler in the Grand National), though his performance in the Grand Sefton suggests he should handle the track. **The Real Whacker** in first-time visor, went well for a long way but the task under much more testing conditions proved too much for him; led, jumped well in main, went with zest, mistake eighth, headed briefly fifteenth, headed 4 out, ridden after, weakened 3 out, pulled up straight; he wouldn't have been an easy horse to campaign this season, though he's been rather overfaced, the Scottish National perhaps a more realistic option for later in the spring.

Mrs Paddy Power Mares' Chase (Liberthine) (Grade 2) (1)

Pos	*Btn*	*Horse*	*Age*	*Wgt*	*Eq*	*Trainer*	*Jockey*	*SP*
1		LIMERICK LACE (IRE)	7	11-2		Gavin Patrick Cromwell, Ireland	Keith Donoghue	3/1
2	¾	DINOBLUE (FR)	7	11-7		W. P. Mullins, Ireland	M. P. Walsh	15/8f
3	5½	MARSH WREN	8	11-2		Stuart Edmunds	Ciaran Gethings	28/1
4	nk	ALLEGORIE DE VASSY (FR)	7	11-5	(t)	W. P. Mullins, Ireland	P. Townend	5/2
5	10	INSTIT (FR)	6	11-2		W. P. Mullins, Ireland	D. E. Mullins	18/1
6	5	RIVIERE D'ETEL (FR)	7	11-2		Gordon Elliott, Ireland	J. W. Kennedy	7/1
7	3	HARMONYA MAKER (FR)	7	11-5		Gordon Elliott, Ireland	Jordan Colin Gainford	40/1
8	14	KESTREL VALLEY	10	11-2	(t)	Nigel Twiston-Davies	Sam Twiston-Davies	100/1
9	½	PINK LEGEND	10	11-2		Venetia Williams	Charlie Deutsch	33/1

9 ran Race Time 5m 35.80 Closing Sectional (3.84f): 62.4s (100.4%) Winning Owner: Mr John P. McManus

The trio at the head of the betting were a little way clear on ratings and 2 of those—in the same ownership—had it to themselves from soon after 2 out, the winner obtaining first run which proved crucial, as did the 5 lb she was getting from the runner-up; this running was a borderline smart one, more on a par with 2022 than last year, but that doesn't mean the principals aren't an extremely likeable pair. **Limerick Lace** belied market weakness and followed up 11 weeks on from another successful raid on these shores, her only defeat this season coming in a top-end handicap, though it would more than likely have been a different story had the favourite been ridden more positively, Limerick Lace able to get first run on her rival; in touch, typically travelled well, slow fifth, pressed leader 4 out, led under pressure entering straight, at least 2 lengths clear when lost momentum last, flashed tail briefly soon after, closed down final 100 yds, always holding on; she's entered in the Grand National and, although she's yet to race beyond 3m, her brother was successful in a stamina-sapping Kim Muir the previous day which offers hope of staying long distances, needing only a handful of omissions to be guaranteed a run. **Dinoblue** back against just her own sex after finishing in front of the Champion Chase 1-2 last time, was conceding upwards of 2 lb all round but still went like the best horse at the weights, conceding first run under a change of tactics attempting this trip for the first time over fences; patiently ridden, not always fluent, smooth headway 4 out, pushed along approaching straight, around 3 lengths down when steadied into 2 out, stayed on. **Marsh Wren** arrived in the form of her life and excelled herself up in grade behind a pair who are already well established in graded company, faring by far the best of the home-trained trio; pressed leader, led eleventh, headed entering straight, no extra between last 2; she's most likeable and genuine, and a credit to connections. **Allegorie de Vassy** who'd finished second when favourite in last year's renewal, failed to justify support back up in trip, the form of her Naas win rather let down in this, and consistency hasn't been a strong point of hers this season; in rear, untidy tenth, jumped right 3 out, crept closer before next, driven there, plugged on. **Instit** was backed at long odds with usual hood left off but is merely ticking over at present; led, headed eleventh, remained prominent, ridden home turn, weakening when steadied into 2 out. **Riviere d'Etel** failed to meet expectations returned to a left-handed track; raced wide/off the pace, typically jumped right, some headway 3 out, left behind early in straight (not persevered with once held). **Harmonya Maker** wasn't up to the task, all her wins when going the other way around in any case; mid-division, jumped none too fluently, driven 3 out, dropped away before next. **Kestrel Valley** was out of depth; taken wide, handy, lost place approaching eleventh, not fluent there, awkward next, lost touch before 3 out. **Pink Legend** had been placed in this race for the last 2 years but ran a shocker for the second successive start, backing out of it quickly; mid-field, struggling badly 5 out.

TIMEFORM'S BEST OF 2023/24

Like much else during the 2023/24 season, the inaugural Timeform Awards for the jumps were monopolised by one man - Willie Mullins. His horses won all five categories that were decided on ratings, with top chaser Galopin des Champs also voted overall Horse of The Season. There's nothing new about Mullins' domination of course—he was champion trainer in Ireland for the eighteenth time—but his latest Irish title was gained with another new record number of winners in a season. All those titles translate to thousands of winners and, at the Punchestown Festival, Mullins overtook Dermot Weld to become Ireland's most successful trainer of all time by that measure. But it wasn't just in Ireland, where he also won all eight Grade 1 races at the Dublin Racing Festival, that Mullins proved all-conquering last season. The leading trainer again at the Cheltenham Festival, where he won the Champion Hurdle and Gold Cup, he also trained his hundredth Festival winner when Jasmin de Vaux took the Champion Bumper under son Patrick. Nine winners in all at Cheltenham, one short of his record there, put Mullins in a position to make a serious bid for the trainers' championship in Britain. I Am Maximus boosted that challenge by winning the Grand National so that, eight years after going so close, in another championship tussle which went down to the final day of the season, Mullins became the first Irish trainer to be champion jumps trainer in Britain since Vincent O'Brien 70 years earlier. While Dan Skelton was therefore denied a first trainers' title, he came out on top in his battle with former boss Paul Nicholls to be the leading British-based trainer, though the latter had the consolation of stable jockey Harry Cobden becoming champion for the first time.

Staying chasers

Galopin des Champs (179) retained his position as the best staying chaser around and matched the achievement of Willie Mullins' other Gold Cup winner Al Boum Photo by successfully defending his Cheltenham title in March. He was the first odds-on Gold Cup winner since Best Mate completed his hat-trick in 2004 and he will be bidding for a third win himself next season after beating second favourite **Gerri Colombe** (172) by three and a half lengths. At Leopardstown over the winter, Galopin des Champs had given a much sounder beating to Gerri Colombe in the Savills Chase and had then won a second Irish Gold Cup on the way to Cheltenham. Gerri Colombe had returned with a narrow win in the Champion Chase at Down Royal on his reappearance and ended his campaign with victory in the Bowl at Aintree from the previous season's runner-up **Ahoy Senor** (166x). **Fastorslow** (173+) unseated in the Cheltenham Gold Cup but proved a thorn in Galopin des Champs' side on more than one occasion. He had a ring-rusty Galopin des Champs back in third in the John Durkan Memorial Punchestown Chase in November and lowered his colours for the second year running in the Punchestown Gold Cup where the emphasis on speed again suited Fastorslow the better. However, the four and a half lengths which separated Galopin des Champs and Fastorslow in the Irish Gold Cup was a better reflection of how the pair measure up. **L'Homme Presse** (170) returned from over a year off to win the Fleur de Lys Chase

Galopin des Champs made it back-to-back victories in the Cheltenham Gold Cup

at Lingfield from subsequent Ryanair Chase winner **Protektorat** (168) and shaped better than the result when fourth in the Gold Cup after making his effort earlier than ideal, losing third to **Corach Rambler** (164). **Shishkin** (167§) would have been one of Britain's best Gold Cup hopes after unluckily departing two out when looking in control of the King George (won by **Hewick** (165) from 2022 winner **Bravemansgame** (164)) and then winning the Denman Chase. However, he was among some notable Nicky Henderson-trained absentees at Cheltenham on account of the stable's form, and he later sadly sustained a fatal injury in his box ahead of an intended run at the Punchestown Festival. **I Am Maximus** (167) put up the best performance by a Grand National winner this century, beating 20 other finishers in a race where 2023 winner Corach Rambler, who was one of just seven British-trained horses lining up in a field with a reduced safety limit, unseated at the first. **Conflated** (167) and **Envoi Allen** (166) failed to win but were both placed in the Champion Chase at Down Royal and in the Ryanair, while Conflated fared the better of the pair when a good second in the Melling Chase at Aintree. **Royale Pagaille** (162) added to his fine record at Haydock when beating the odds-on Bravemansgame in the Betfair Chase in which Corach Rambler and Protektorat also under-performed.

Two-mile chasers

It was all change at the head of the two-mile chase division. Energumene, winner of the previous two Queen Mother Champion Chases, was on the sidelines, and it was the one-two from the 2023 Arkle, **El Fabiolo** (174) and **Jonbon** (172), who were the two best performers.

However, it wasn't until the final day of the British season that the pair actually met again, with El Fabiolo redirected from Punchestown to help in Mullins' British title bid. But while the strong-travelling Jonbon ended his season on a high note to win the Celebration Chase for the second year running, the odds-on El Fabiolo, four lengths back in second, failed to fire with his jumping not as slick as the winner's. El Fabiolo's jumping had let him down to a greater degree in the Queen Mother Champion Chase, where he seemed to have a golden opportunity (sent off 2/9) in Jonbon's absence, but a serious mistake at the fifth gave Paul Townend little option but to pull him up. That ended El Fabiolo's unbeaten record over fences, but he'd earlier put up top-class performances to land very short odds in the Hilly Way Chase at Cork and the Dublin Chase at Leopardstown. Jonbon too came unstuck at very short odds at an earlier Cheltenham meeting, when turned over by the Haldon Gold Cup winner **Elixir de Nutz** (158) in the rearranged Clarence House Chase at Cheltenham, but that was his only blip in a season in which he won the Shloer Chase, Tingle Creek Chase and Melling Chase on a first try at two and a half miles, as well as the Celebration Chase, taking his wonderfully consistent career record to 14 wins and 3 seconds from 17 starts. A three-finisher Champion Chase was fought out instead by the previous season's runner-up **Captain Guinness** (164) and El Fabiolo's stablemate **Gentleman de Mee** (161), both of those beaten in the Dublin Chase where the mare **Dinoblue** (156), winner of the Paddy's Rewards Club Chase from

Captain Guinness gained his Grade 1 breakthrough in the Champion Chase

Gentleman de Mee, had finished runner-up to El Fabiolo. After finishing second to **Limerick Lace** (147+) in the Mares' Chase at Cheltenham, Dinoblue was a short price for the Champion Chase at Punchestown in El Fabiolo's absence but was only third behind **Banbridge** (165), winner of the Silviniaco Conti Chase at Kempton earlier in the season, who beat Captain Guinness a neck. **Edwardstone** (164) remained one of the top two-mile chasers in Britain, winning the Game Spirit Chase by a wide margin but otherwise chasing home Jonbon in the Shloer and Tingle Creek and finishing third behind him in the Celebration Chase. He would have picked up place money too in the Champion Chase had he not fallen two out. **Boothill** (160) began the season winning a couple of valuable handicaps at Ascot before falling in the Desert Orchid Chase (run as a handicap for the first time and won for the second year running by the unpredictable **Editeur du Gite** (157§)) and Game Spirit, but he proved at least as good as ever when beaten around seven lengths in fourth in the Celebration Chase.

Novice chasers

Last season's novices were a strong crop and look sure to make their mark in open company in 2024/25, none more so than **Gaelic Warrior** (169) who was the pick of them. A smart hurdler, he gained his first Grade 1 win over fences when making all in the Faugheen Novice Chase at Limerick just after Christmas but ran his best race in a first-time hood when dropped back in trip to win the Arkle with a polished performance which gives him plenty of options this season. Over longer trips, stablemate **Fact To File** (166p) looks at least as good a prospect and very much a Gold Cup contender after impressing on his first try over three miles in the Brown Advisory Novices' Chase at Cheltenham which he won from **Monty's Star** (156). That was Fact To File's second Grade 1 success after coming home alone in a match against Gaelic Warrior at the Dublin Racing Festival where the latter was already beaten when unseating at the last. A third Mullins novice, the Irish Arkle winner **Il Etait Temps** (164), had finished placed behind Gaelic Warrior at both Limerick and Cheltenham but turned the tables on his stablemate who wasn't at his best at Punchestown. Il Etait Temps had also taken the scalps of the two leading British-trained novices in the Manifesto Novices' Chase at Aintree; **Grey Dawning** (160) had reversed earlier Cheltenham form with **Ginny's Destiny** (158) when beating that rival in the Turners' Novices Chase but they finished the other way round again behind Il Etait Temps at Aintree. Besides Fact To File and I Am Maximus (winner of the Drinmore when still eligible for novices earlier in the season), JP McManus has a formidable team of young staying chasers which also includes the wide-margin National Hunt Novices' Chase winner **Corbetts Cross** (164), later a fine third in the Bowl at Aintree, the Mildmay Novices' Chase winner **Inothewayurthinkin** (158p), who had earlier landed a gamble in the Fulke Walwyn Kim Muir at Cheltenham, and **Spillane's Tower** (158p), a Grade 1 winner in the spring at both Fairyhouse and Punchestown (Monty's Star runner-up again), all of those with different Irish yards. Gordon Elliott's consistent **Found A Fifty** (158) had to settle for second in the Drinmore and again in the Arkle at both Leopardstown and Cheltenham, but he also picked up a couple of Grade 1 wins, in the final running of the Racing Post Novice Chase at Leopardstown's Christmas meeting and in the Maghull Novices' Chase at Aintree when a head winner from the Wayward Lad Novices' Chase winner **Master Chewy** (156) who had been running respectably when falling in the Arkle. The other very smart novice to mention is **Grangeclare West** (159p) who had Corbetts Cross behind him when winning both his starts but missed the rest of the season after getting cast in his box, having won the Neville Hotels Novice Chase at Leopardstown in December with plenty of authority.

Staying hurdlers

The staying hurdle division lacked quality but was at least fairly competitive and had a worthy leader in **Teahupoo** (163). A close third in the Stayers' Hurdle in 2023, he went two places better this time having been kept fresh since gaining a second successive win in the Hatton's Grace Hurdle at Fairyhouse in December from Impaire Et Passe. Teahupoo ended an unbeaten campaign by winning the Champion Stayers Hurdle at Punchestown from **Asterion Forlonge** (155) who'd been sixth behind him at Cheltenham, though that was a bittersweet success for Gordon Elliott with 2023 Stayers' Hurdle winner **Sire du Berlais** (152), fifth in the latest edition, sustaining a fatal injury. Irish-trained horses dominated the Stayers' Hurdle, with the former dual winner **Flooring Porter** (159), who began the season over fences, finishing second ahead of **Home By The Lee** (157) in third, his best placing on his third attempt at the race and one he replicated at Punchestown. 40/1 shot **Buddy One** (154), who'd graduated from handicaps, completed the frame at both Cheltenham and Punchestown and in between fared best of a strong Irish team in the Liverpool Hurdle at Aintree where he finished second ahead of the lightly-raced Boyne Hurdle winner **Hiddenvalley Lake** (154). The new name who emerged to win at Aintree was **Strong Leader** (158) who'd skipped the Stayers' Hurdle but should be a leading player in the staying division from now on for Olly Murphy, being totally unexposed over three miles. **Crambo** (153) looked another younger British-trained contender for top honours in the spring after narrowly denying **Paisley Park** (153) what would have been a fourth success in the Long Walk Hurdle but proved disappointing at both Cheltenham and Aintree. Paisley Park was also narrowly beaten by former Grand National winner **Noble Yeats** (150) when bidding for a fourth win in the Cleeve Hurdle, conceding weight to the winner and third-placed Strong Leader. He was retired after contesting his sixth Stayers' Hurdle, a race he'd won in 2019. Leopardstown's Christmas Hurdle winner Irish Point and Home By The Lee were among the Irish raiders in the Grande Course de Haies d'Auteuil but it was a couple better known over fences who fared best of the visitors, with **Hewick** (154) making the frame for the second year running to finish runner-up and **Mahler Mission** (153) in fourth.

Two-mile hurdlers

Instead of a novice chase campaign, **Constitution Hill** (177) remained over hurdles in a bid to retain his Champion Hurdle crown but in the event he was seen out only once, making short work of just smart rivals at best in the Christmas Hurdle at Kempton for the second year running. He missed an intended run beforehand in the Fighting Fifth Hurdle, which was delayed by a week and run on heavy ground at Sandown, while a bad scope ruled Constitution Hill out of the International Hurdle, in its new slot on Cheltenham's Trials Day, and he missed the Champion Hurdle too after a disappointing racecourse gallop at Kempton

Paul Townend celebrates State Man's victory in the Champion Hurdle

which turned out to be indicative of issues affecting Nicky Henderson's string more widely at the time. Constitution Hill's absence from the Champion Hurdle hardly made the race any less one-sided, however, with the previous year's runner-up **State Man** (167) taking the opportunity to add the Cheltenham race to another clean sweep of Ireland's top two-mile hurdles—the Morgiana, Matheson, Irish Champion and Punchestown Champion Hurdle, all of which he'd also won the previous season. State Man's second to Constitution Hill in the 2023 Champion Hurdle remains his only defeat in completed starts since joining Willie Mullins and his number of Grade 1 wins now stands at ten. The first Champion Hurdle run on heavy ground since the 1980s, it was badly short on depth, like the division as a whole, with **Irish Point** (163), who was rerouted from the Stayers' Hurdle (after winning the Christmas Hurdle at Leopardstown), faring best of the rest and also finishing runner-up to State Man at Punchestown. Completing the frame in the Champion Hurdle were Constitution Hill's stablemate **Luccia** (152), winner of a premier handicap at Ascot on her previous start, and the Galway Hurdle and Limestone Lad Hurdle winner **Zarak The Brave** (154), while the Welsh Champion Hurdle and Kingwell Hurdle winner **Nemean Lion** (153) and veteran **Not So Sleepy** (148), who'd won the rearranged Fighting Fifth, were the last two finishers. Champion Hurdle hopes for **Impaire Et Passe** (162) were dented by a couple of defeats behind stablemate State Man but he fared better stepped up to two and a half miles in the spring, winning the Aintree Hurdle in a three-way finish with Lismullen Hurdle and

Relkeel Hurdle winner **Bob Olinger** (159) and Coral Cup winner **Langer Dan** (159). He beat Langer Dan again in the Select Hurdle at Sandown. **Lossiemouth** (154) would be a welcome addition to the Champion Hurdle field for Mullins this season as she took her record to eight wins from nine starts with odds-on victories in the International Hurdle and the Grade 1 mares' hurdles at both Cheltenham and Punchestown. For the second year running, **Pied Piper** (156) put up a very smart performance to be placed under a big weight in the County Hurdle, having changed hands for €570,000 the previous month.

Novice hurdlers

In common with the other divisions, Irish domination was largely the theme among the novice hurdlers with **Ballyburn** (162p) proving the best of them and looking a most exciting prospect, making appeal as a future chaser. Beaten only on his hurdling debut, Ballyburn ran up a Grade 1 hat-trick, dropping back to two miles at the Dublin Racing Festival but then returning to further to impressively win the Gallagher Novices' Hurdle, in which Mullins trained the first five. He signed off by winning at very short odds in the two-and-a-half mile Champion Novice Hurdle at Punchestown. Stablemate **Mystical Power** (153) won Punchestown's KPMG Champion Novice Hurdle over two miles and looks more likely to remain over hurdles, in keeping with his breeding, by Galileo out of Champion Hurdle winner Annie Power. Also the winner of the Moscow Flyer Novice Hurdle at Punchestown in the winter, Mystical Power was runner-up in the Supreme Novices' at Cheltenham but went one better in the Top Novices' Hurdle at Aintree. **Slade Steel** (152) was no match for Ballyburn at the Dublin Racing Festival but outstayed Mystical Power to win the Supreme. He could

Ballyburn proved he was the best in the division with a wide-margin win in the Gallagher Novices' Hurdle

only finish third to Mystical Power at Punchestown when tending to jump left. **Firefox** (151) beat Ballyburn when they made their hurdling debuts at Fairyhouse in December, and while he didn't add to that win, he ran consistently in the best company afterwards, finishing third to Slade Steel in the Supreme and runner-up to Mystical Power at both Aintree and Punchestown. He's another who's very much a chaser on looks. **Dancing City** (148) was third in the Albert Bartlett Novices' Hurdle at Cheltenham but that was his only defeat at the big festivals as he won the Nathaniel Lacy & Partners Solicitors Novice Hurdle at Leopardstown, the Sefton Novices' at Aintree and a deep renewal of the War of Attrition Novice Hurdle at Punchestown where stablemate **High Class Hero** (145), the Martin Pipe winner **Better Days Ahead** (146) and the Albert Bartlett winner **Stellar Story** (147) completed the frame. Stellar Story had got up in the last strides to pip **The Jukebox Man** (147) in the Albert Bartlett, with the latter also runner-up to Dancing City in the Sefton at Aintree. Another smart effort from a Mullins-trained novice at Punchestown came from **Daddy Long Legs** (149p) who comfortably beat a big field in a listed two-mile handicap. Both Daddy Long Legs and his stablemate **Absurde** (146p), the subsequent County Hurdle winner, had contested the Future Champions Novice Hurdle at Leopardstown just after Christmas which was won by **Caldwell Potter** (147p) who was following in the footsteps of his brother Mighty Potter two years earlier. Later sold from Gordon Elliott for a record €740,000 to join Paul Nicholls, Caldwell Potter missed his intended debut for new connections in the Mersey Novices' Hurdle at Aintree but is one to look forward to over fences. Coincidentally, the Mersey was won by Caldwell Potter's half-sister and former stablemate **Brighterdaysahead** (139p) who met with an odds-on defeat at Cheltenham but won her other races in the manner of a very promising mare. Nicky Henderson's **Jango Baie** (148p) won the first running of the Grade 1 Formby Novices' Hurdle (replacing Sandown's Tolworth) at Aintree's new Boxing Day fixture and ran his best race afterwards when finishing strongly for second after meeting trouble in running in a premier handicap at the Grand National meeting. Henderson also had the season's leading juvenile hurdler **Sir Gino** (153p) who had to miss the Cheltenham Festival but kept his unbeaten record when beating the Triumph Hurdle runner-up **Kargese** (142) in the Anniversary Juvenile Hurdle at Aintree. Kargese won both of Ireland's Grade 1 juvenile contests at Leopardstown and Punchestown but, with Mullins fielding seven in the Triumph, she was beaten by stablemate **Majborough** (150p) at Cheltenham, the winner an exciting prospect for chasing who had been third to Kargese on his Irish debut in the Spring Juvenile.

2023/24 STATISTICS (Britain)

TRAINERS (1,2,3 earnings)		Horses	Indiv'l Wnrs	Races Won	Runs	% Strike Rate	Stakes £
1	W. P. Mullins, Ireland	115	26	28	160	17.5	3,119,001
2	Paul Nicholls	169	92	132	564	23.4	2,775,472
3	Dan Skelton	210	74	120	783	15.3	2,774,423
4	Nicky Henderson	144	60	91	440	20.7	2,129,600
5	Gordon Elliott, Ireland	102	17	20	138	14.5	1,470,444
6	Venetia Williams	85	35	57	337	16.9	1,383,209
7	Olly Murphy	135	62	102	461	22.1	1,203,968
8	Ben Pauling	123	47	76	438	17.4	1,143,909
9	Nigel Twiston-Davies	104	49	78	435	17.9	1,074,307
10	Fergal O'Brien	171	68	107	537	19.9	1,071,837

JOCKEYS (by winners)		1st	2nd	3rd	Unpl	Total Rides	% Strike Rate
1	Harry Cobden	164	131	95	346	736	22.3
2	Sean Bowen	157	122	84	359	722	21.7
3	Brian Hughes	122	118	106	410	756	16.1
4	Sam Twiston-Davies	103	107	98	334	642	16.0
5	Gavin Sheehan	91	76	67	310	544	16.7
6	Harry Skelton	81	74	67	201	423	19.1
7	Nico de Boinville	59	32	32	131	254	23.2
8	Jonjo O'Neill Jr.	56	49	45	229	379	14.8
9	Ben Jones	55	56	49	176	336	16.4
10	James Bowen	52	55	55	190	352	14.8

SIRES OF WINNERS (1,2,3 earnings)		Races Won	Runs	% Strike Rate	Stakes £
1	Walk In The Park (by Montjeu)	78	541	14.4	1,756,287
2	Kayf Tara (by Sadler's Wells)	95	535	17.8	1,377,664
3	Flemensfirth (by Alleged)	62	422	14.7	1,132,131
4	Fame And Glory (by Montjeu)	76	492	15.4	1,111,617
5	Getaway (by Monsun)	104	825	12.6	1,071,070
6	Shantou (by Alleged)	58	383	15.1	1,018,226
7	Yeats (by Sadler's Wells)	56	519	10.8	983,975
8	Westerner (by Danehill)	60	473	12.7	981,045
9	Mahler (by Galileo)	79	570	13.9	964,419
10	Saint Des Saints (by Cadoudal)	22	170	12.9	948,519

LEADING HORSES (1,2,3 earnings)		Races Won	Runs	Stakes £
1	I Am Maximus 7 b.g Authorized - Polysheba	1	1	500,000
2	Jonbon 7 b.g Walk In The Park - Star Face	5	4	442,798
3	Galopin Des Champs 7 bl.g Timos - Manon Des Champs	1	1	357,938
4	Protektorat 8 b.g Saint Des Saints - Protektion	6	1	304,036
5	Gerri Colombe 7 b.g Saddler Maker - Ruse De Guerre	2	1	276,175
6	Captain Guinness 8 b.g Arakan - Presenting D'Azy	1	1	266,240
7	State Man 6 ch.g Doctor Dino - Arret Station	1	1	263,662
8	Delta Work 10 br.g Network - Robbe	2	0	200,000
9	Grey Dawning 6 gr.g Flemensfirth - Lady Wagtail	6	3	198,275
10	Impaire Et Passe 5 b.g Diamond Boy - Brune Ecossaise	2	2	186,635

SECTION 5

THE TIMEFORM TOP 100

Hurdlers

177	Constitution Hill
167	State Man
163	Klassical Dream
163	Teahupoo
162	Ballyburn
162	Goa Lil
162	Impaire Et Passe
161	Irish Point
160	Appreciate It
160	Sire du Berlais
160	Vauban
159	Bob Olinger
158	Facile Vega
158	Sharjah
158	Strong Leader
158§	Commander of Fleet
157	Flooring Porter
157	Home By The Lee
157	Il Est Francais
157x	Zanahiyr
156	Gold Tweet
156	Langer Dan
156	Pied Piper
155	Asterion Forlonge
155	The Storyteller
154p	Lossiemouth
154	Buddy One
154	Gaelic Warrior
154	Hewick
154	Hiddenvalley Lake
154	Jesse Evans
154	Knappers Hill
154	Zarak The Brave
153p	Sir Gino
153p	The Nice Guy
153	Blazing Khal
153	Crambo
153	Hooligan
153	Mahler Mission
153	Mcfabulous
153	Mystical Power
153	Paisley Park
152	Blueking d'Oroux
152	Brewin'upastorm
152	El Fabiolo
152	James du Berlais
152	Minella Cocooner
152	Saint Roi
152	Slade Steel
152	Winter Fog
151	Concertista
151	Darasso
151	Firefox
151	Maxxum
151	Meet And Greet
151	Saldier
151	Sir Gerhard
150p	Majborough
150	Ballyadam
150	Gentlemansgame
150	Henri Le Farceur
150	Inthepocket
150	Rubaud
150	Saint Sam
149p	Mister Policeman
149+	Daddy Long Legs
149	Ashdale Bob
149	Beauport
149	Brentford Hope
149	Champ Kiely
149	Colonel Mustard
149	Epatante
149	Farouk d'Alene
149	Fastorslow
149	Il Etait Temps
149	Nemean Lion
149	Nurburgring
149	Quel Destin
149	Scaramanga
148p	Jango Baie
148	Botox Has
148	Dancing City
148	Dashel Drasher
148	Fil Dor
148	Flame Bearer
148	French Dynamite
148	Good Land
148	Luccia
148	Monkfish
148	My Mate Mozzie
148	Noble Yeats
148	Not So Sleepy
148	Quilixios
148	Tommy's Oscar
148§	Goshen
147p	Caldwell Potter
147	Champ
147	Filey Bay
147	Stellar Story
147	Thedevilscoachman
147	The Jukebox Man

Chasers

180	Energumene
179	Galopin des Champs
174	El Fabiolo
173+	Fastorslow
172	Gerri Colombe
172	Jonbon
170	L'Homme Presse
169	Gaelic Warrior
168	Protektorat
167	Conflated
167	I Am Maximus
167§	Shishkin
166p	Fact To File
166	Envoi Allen
166x	Ahoy Senor
165	Banbridge
165	Hewick
164	Bravemansgame
164	Captain Guinness
164	Clan des Obeaux
164	Corach Rambler
164	Corbetts Cross
164	Edwardstone
164	Gentlemansgame
164	Greaneteen
164	Il Etait Temps
164	Stage Star
164?	Noble Yeats
163+	Ferny Hollow
163	Allaho
163	Blue Lord
163	Journey With Me
163	Pic d'Orhy
163	Tornado Flyer
163?	Appreciate It
162	Bachasson
162	Royale Pagaille
161	Gentleman de Mee
161	Haddex des Obeaux
161	Minella Indo
160	Boothill
160	Delta Work
160	First Flow
160	Grey Dawning
160	Sounds Russian
160x	Capodanno
160?	Bob Olinger
159p	Grangeclare West
159p	Impervious
159+	Feronily
159	Coko Beach
159	Easy Game
159	Jungle Boogie
159	Kilcruit
158p	Inothewayurthinkin
158p	Spillane's Tower
158	Dashel Drasher
158	Elixir de Nutz
158	Fakir d'Oudairies
158	Found A Fifty
158	Ginny's Destiny
158	Master McShee
158	Nassalam
158	Saint Sam
158	The Big Dog
158	Tommy's Oscar
158x	Saint Roi
158?	Monkfish
157	Ash Tree Meadow
157	Datsalrightgino
157	Franco de Port
157	Galvin
157	Hang In There
157	Il Est Francais
157	Mahler Mission
157	Melon
157	Thunder Rock
157§	Editeur du Gite

157§	Hitman
156+	Sir Gerhard
156	Dinoblue
156	Gaillard du Mesnil
156	Haut En Couleurs
156	Master Chewy
156	Monty's Star
156	Notlongtillmay
156	Paint The Dream
156	Stolen Silver
156x	Asterion Forlonge
156?	Fil Dor
156§	Chantry House
155p	Marine Nationale
155	Ga Law
155	Midnight River
155	Minella Cocooner
155	Pencilfulloflead
155	Stay Away Fay
155x	Beacon Edge
154p	Iroko
154	Hercule du Seuil

Juvenile Hurdlers

153p	Sir Gino
150p	Majborough
149	Nurburgring
142	Kargese
141	Bottler'secret
141	Salver
140	Storm Heart
139p	Salvator Mundi
138	Eastern Legend
138	Kalif du Berlais
137	Bunting
137	Ndaawi
136	Ethical Diamond
135	Burdett Road
135	Intellotto
134	Kala Conti
132	Givemefive
132	Harsh
132	Karl des Tourelles
131p	Kabral du Mathan
131	Eagle Fang
131	Lark In The Mornin
131	Mordor
130p	Trustyourinstinct
130	Batman Girac
130	Wodhooh
129	Highwind
129?	Mighty Bandit
128	Miss Manzor
128	Pigeon House

Novice Hurdlers

162	Ballyburn
153	Mystical Power
152	Slade Steel
151	Firefox
149+	Daddy Long Legs
148p	Jango Baie
148	Dancing City
147p	Caldwell Potter
147	Stellar Story
147	The Jukebox Man
146p	Absurde
146	Better Days Ahead
145	High Class Hero
144p	Quai de Bourbon
144	July Flower
144	Tullyhill
143p	Brighterdaysahead
143p	Favour And Fortune
143	Asian Master
143	The Wallpark
142	Jimmy du Seuil
142	Mistergif
142?	Encanto Bruno
141	Dee Capo
141	Farren Glory
141	Ile Atlantique
141	King of Kingsfield
141	Readin Tommy Wrong
140	Harvard Guy
140	Shannon Royale

Novice Chasers

169	Gaelic Warrior
166p	Fact To File
164	Corbetts Cross
164	Il Etait Temps
160	Grey Dawning
159p	Grangeclare West
158p	Inothewayurthinkin
158p	Spillane's Tower
158	Found A Fifty
158	Ginny's Destiny
157	Il Est Francais
156	Master Chewy
156	Monty's Star
155p	Marine Nationale
155	Minella Cocooner
155	Stay Away Fay
154p	Iroko
154	Facile Vega
154	Hercule du Seuil
153	Giovinco
153	Heart Wood
152	Blood Destiny
152	Hunters Yarn
151	Chianti Classico
151	Hermes Allen
151	Letsbeclearaboutit
151	My Mate Mozzie
151	Salvador Ziggy
150	Broadway Boy
150	Three Card Brag

National Hunt Flat Horses

126	Redemption Day
125	A Dream To Share
122	Jasmin de Vaux
119	Romeo Coolio
118	The Yellow Clay
118	Wingmen
116	Jalon d'Oudairies
116	Queensbury Boy
115	Jeroboam Machin
115	William Munny
114	Sounds Victorius
113	Fishery Lane
113	Horaces Pearl
112	Brechin Castle
112	Crest of Glory
112	Tripoli Flyer
112	You Oughta Know
110p	Kopek des Bordes
110	Good And Clever
110	Harbour Highway
110	Shuttle Diplomacy
110	The Enabler
109	Diva Luna
108p	Potters Charm
108	Cantico
108	Junta Marvel
108	Mister Meggit
108	Mount Bonete
108	Mozzies Sister
108	Regent's Stroll
108	Sole Solution

Index

A

B

C

D

E

F

G

H

I

J

K

L

M

Index To Photographers

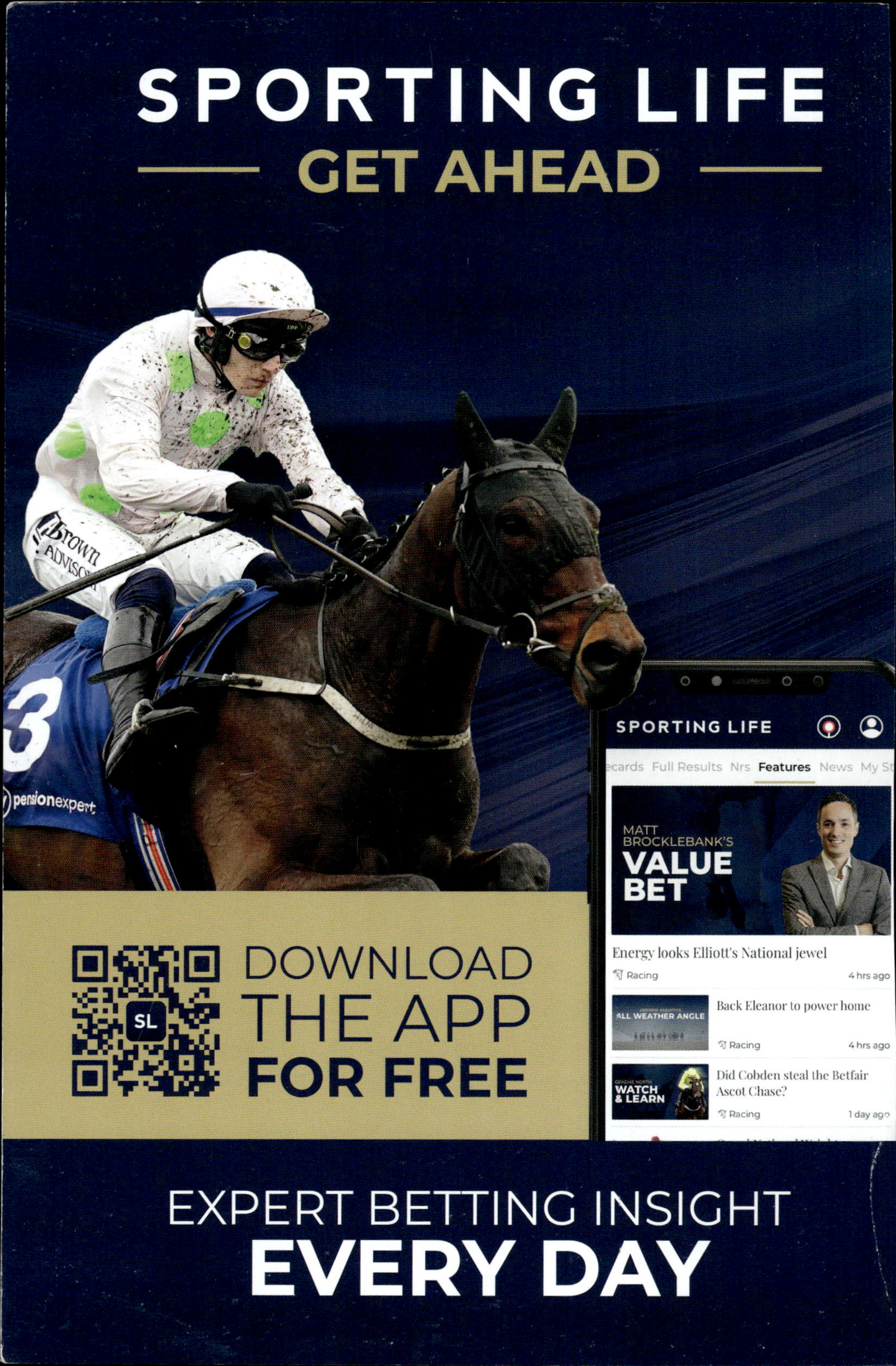
SPORTING LIFE
GET AHEAD
Brown
ADVISORY
3
pensionexpert
SPORTING LIFE
ecards Full Results Nrs Features News My St
MATT BROCKLEBANK'S
VALUE BET
Energy looks Elliott's National jewel
Racing
4 hrs ago
ALL WEATHER ANGLE
Back Eleanor to power home
Racing
4 hrs ago
WATCH & LEARN
Did Cobden steal the Betfair Ascot Chase?
Racing
1 day ago
SL
DOWNLOAD
THE APP
FOR FREE
EXPERT BETTING INSIGHT
EVERY DAY